Texas Politicians
Good 'n' Bad

Mona D. Sizer

Texas Politicians
Good 'n' Bad

Mona D. Sizer

Republic of Texas Press

Library of Congress Cataloging-in-Publication Data

Sizer, Mona D.
  Texas politicians: good 'n' bad / Mona D. Sizer.
     p. cm.
  Includes bibliographical references and index.
  ISBN 1-55622-876-7
  1. Politicians--Texas--Biography. 2. Texas--Biography. 3. Texas--Politics and government. I. Title.

F385 .S59 2001   2001041903
976.4'009'9--dc21   CIP

© 2002, Mona D. Sizer
All Rights Reserved

Republic of Texas Press is an imprint of Wordware Publishing, Inc.
No part of this book may be reproduced in any form or by
any means without permission in writing from
Wordware Publishing, Inc.

Printed in the United States of America

ISBN 1-55622-876-7
10 9 8 7 6 5 4 3 2 1
0801

All inquiries for volume purchases of this book should be addressed to Wordware Publishing, Inc., at 2320 Los Rios Boulevard, Plano, Texas 75074. Telephone inquiries may be made by calling:
(972) 423-0090

Contents

Acknowledgments ix
Part I: Strange Bedfellows. 1
   The Greatest Good For All 3
   "The Freewheeling, Loose-scrupled Liberal"
   James Edward Ferguson 7
      Early Years 7
      The Farm Problem 12
      Farmer Jim 15
      History's Assessment 22
   "The Sunbonnet Governor"
   Miriam Amanda Wallace Ferguson 23
      Running For Election 23
      Governing the State 34
      History's Summation 44
   "The Duke of Duval"
   George Berham Parr 47
      The Way *It* Worked 47
      The Heir Apparent 52
      Payback Time 57
      The Glare of the Spotlight 61
      The Gloves Come Off 64
      Strange Bedfellows Indeed 67
      The Wheels of the Gods 69
      Ride the Man Down 70
      History's Assessment 72

Contents

"The Consummate Politician"
Lyndon Baines Johnson 73
    The Dealing for the Presidency 73
    Texas in His Bones 78
    The Ins and Outs. 83
    Winning in the War. 88
    The Ambition To Be Great. 92
    The Bit in His Teeth 98
    The New Job 105
    The Pinnacle of Power 112
    Not With a Bang 117
    History's Assessment. 120

Part II: Hot Oil 121
    Taming the Wild Beast 123

"The Great Regulator"
James Stephen Hogg 129
    Taming the Captains of Industry 129
    From Spindletop to Swindletop 140
    The Rush for Black Gold 148

"The Standard Oil Senator"
Joseph Weldon Bailey 155
    Big Oil Comes to the Party 155
    Too Hot to Handle 164

"The Oilman as Politician"
Ross Shaw Sterling. 171
    Anything to Beat Ma Ferguson 171
    East Texas Blows In 179
    The Hot Oil War 187
    "Here Comes The Law!" 190

The Hot Oil War Goes National 197
    The Governor at Bay—James V Allred 197
    The Tide Turns—Robert Allan Shivers 206
    What Windfall Profits? 216

The Hot Oil War Goes International 223
    George Herbert Walker Bush—
    the Hot Oil President. 223

Bibliography 227

Index. 231

Acknowledgments

Many people aided me in the writing of this book. I would like to acknowledge lifelong friends Ruth and Bob Welch, who offered me their home while I did research.

Likewise, Patricia Buttery lent me books from her extensive library that provided valuable insights and quotations. Thanks to my critique group Marci Fuller, Jan Gracia, and Susie Berberian, who read pages and pages of raw material and through our talks helped me see the pattern of the book as it emerged.

Of course, Ginnie Bivona and Dianne Stultz offered their usual encouragement and suggestions. Their enthusiasm for the project kept me forging ahead. The timeliness of this book while the fourth president from Texas governs in the White House is an added blessing.

The wild and woolly world of politics became a revelation to me. What was known and when it was known were as much points of controversy at the beginning of the twentieth century as they are today.

As with all writing, the author must mine from a rich vein of material the nuggets that the reader will find most intriguing. If my readers are flabbergasted, then I've done my work well.

Mona D. Sizer
Harlingen, Texas

Other titles by Mona D. Sizer

The King Ranch Story: Truth and Myth

"Makes reading about history an enjoyable pursuit."
Eileen Mattei, *Valley Morning Star*

"The legend, the lore, the truth, all woven together."
W. C. Jameson

Texas Heroes: A Dynasty of Courage

"Sizer has chosen men from Texas history to identify as heroic and courageous. Very readable."
Chuck Parsons, *True West*

"An information-filled volume of 13 gallant men whose heroism has made the legends."
Larry Lawrence, *Abilene Reporter News*

"...belongs in every library in the state."
Jim McKone, *The Monitor*

Texas Justice: Bought and Paid For

"...most dramatic because they involve real people. Sizer brings these characters to full view for her readers as well as offering emotions for the victims, without putting words in their mouths."
Tamara Cupples, *Valley Morning Star*

"For those who love true crime, here it is with a Texas twist. An engrossing read."
Doris Meredith, *The Roundup*

Part I

Strange Bedfellows

The Greatest Good For All

Physical distance between Austin, Texas, and Athens, Greece, stretches thousands of miles. The ancient world that produced Greek philosophy, arguably the basis for all modern philosophic thought, stretches even farther across centuries and through at least half a dozen languages both archaic and arcane. Yet the universal truths of the Greeks are the truths of the Texans, who would have understood each other better than either would have thought possible.

In ancient Athens sometime around 375 B.C., Plato detailed the ideal state in *The Republic*. It was to be a government ruled by an ideal philosophy. Politics was one of its five branches—the study of the ideal social organization. It asked the question, "How can men govern other men so that they may achieve the greatest good for all?"

The answer is surprising. The "rights" of man were then as they are today. Realistically they are the "mights" of man. Or so they have always been in the Lone Star State, and so they were in ancient Greece. Draco, Solon, and certainly Pericles were not good by nature. Lyndon Baines Johnson, George Parr, and "Farmer Jim" Ferguson were not good by nature. But each espoused powerful ambitions. And every man's ambition is self-serving. No man unless he is stupid or insane will destroy his own opportunities or damage his chances to achieve wealth or power. Indeed destruction of opportunity to achieve wealth results in the destruction of power, something communist countries in their misery have learned as the twenty-first century dawns.

Politicians and sometimes the men they serve are always aware of opportunities. They are always aware of wealth and power. Their good is anything that adds to their wealth and power. Swiftly they come to realize that their good is irrevocably linked to the good of the people they hope to exploit.

In the beginning they may have no fellow-feeling at all except a vague contempt. Little by little, sympathy comes—for family, for friends, for community, for state. From sympathy comes kindness or an imitation of those feelings because the politician cannot govern successfully without the consent of a considerable number of the governed. He is one. They are many.

From his kindness come traditions for the group. Traditions become proper moral behavior. Gradually, the law of the individual becomes the legal and moral power of the whole.

Whether he wants to be or not, the man who governs for any length of time becomes better than he was when he began, better than he ever thought he could be. He may never realize that he has been molded. He may control his passion and his vice because reason and virtue allow him to take more for himself. He may know himself to be a fake and a ruthless entrepreneur. He may pat himself on the back for fooling everyone.

He is only fooling himself. Only if in taking more for himself, he creates more for everyone, will he be allowed to do so. If his laws and his governance help others to realize more for themselves, then he may be praised by many. He may be loved by a few. He may even be lauded by a handful as a statesman.

Such men were the rough-and-tumble brutes who stepped into the halls of government in Texas. In many cases they were undereducated and only half civilized. Many attained their first elective office while they were still selfish, crooked, brutal, and infinitely dangerous to know. But the good that came out of their rule—directly or indirectly—made them famous beyond their time.

The Greeks would have understood them perfectly.

Miriam Ferguson, the first woman elected governor in Texas, was believed to be a pawn for her husband, who had been impeached. Her plan—if she had one—was to rescind James Ferguson's impeachment so he could run again. The platform they devised for her was a simple one. She was against the Ku Klux Klan. She was for education. While these were laudable and certainly got her elected, a greater good came from her election than anyone had suspected. Some 720,000 Texans voted in 1924 as opposed to 400,000 in 1922. Jim might have told her what to do and what to sign, but Texas led the nation in woman suffrage as women turned out to vote for the first time for *their* representative.

Allan Shivers was determined to save the tidelands of Texas, ostensibly for the schoolchildren, but primarily for the oil industry where he had spent much of his life. He cross-filed to run as a gubernatorial candidate for both the Democrat and Republican parties to elect Dwight Eisenhower, who promptly signed the bill giving the oil rich lands to the states. More important than anyone suspected was the fact that Texas became a two-party state whose opinions, backed by its increasing number of electoral votes, could no longer be neglected by politicians running for national offices.

Lyndon Baines Johnson, the cleverest and most self-serving of Texas politicians, was elevated to the highest office in the land by an assassin's bullet. In the halcyon days that followed his predecessor's death, Johnson managed to enact civil rights legislation that changed America forever. We can only vaguely remember what our lives were like before it.

Such are the men and women who enriched our lives even as they enriched themselves. Flawed they might be, but they stand head and shoulders above the lesser, blander types who preceded and succeeded them to the offices they won.

They fascinate us as examples of the many faces, both good and bad, that one person may wear. One and all they reveled in what they did, emerged richer for the experience, and bettered the lives of the citizens who elected them almost in spite of themselves.

If the goal of politics is to achieve the ideal social organization, we should realize that turning a selective blind eye is one of the accommodations we must make if that goal is to be reached.

"The Freewheeling, Loose-scrupled Liberal"

James Edward Ferguson

"All told, it is generally admitted that my first administration was one of the most successful in the state's history."

Early Years

Jim Ferguson was the sixth child of a circuit-riding Methodist preacher. In 1896 when he was twenty-five years old, he is reputed to have scrawled "Law by God" on the bedroom wall in his mother's farmhouse on the banks of Salado Creek in Bell County, Texas. His decision probably came as a surprise to his parents because he had been a bad boy, dropping out of school, sowing his wild oats, and driving his family to distraction. Until that night when he had been invited to a party. There he met his lovely distant cousin, Miriam Amanda Wallace.

For the occasion she had dressed in a white lace dress with sheer ruffles around her neck and just above her elbows. A wide white sash cinched in her slender waist and hips. Her dark brown hair was done up in the Victorian manner, piled on top of her head in a loose, full style to show off the graceful column of her neck. She was the picture of a rich man's daughter, far above Jim Ferguson's humble and slightly disreputable station.

She may have been polite to him, but she probably passed over him without a second thought. He was a fair-enough looking young man, but so were many others. He was a poor relation with no education and no prospects. She probably never expected to hear from him again.

Where he would have gone and what he would have done with himself if he had not met her is anybody's guess. He'd been a wanderer from job to job since his expulsion for disobedience from Salado College, the local preparatory school. Since the age of twelve, he'd worked as a miner, a bellhop, a vineyard laborer, a roustabout, a teamster, a lumberjack, and a hand on a railroad gang. He'd been a bum. Footloose and without ambition, he'd roamed from Texas to California and back again.

Then that night he saw Miriam Wallace. He wanted her and all that went with her. What he wanted, he was suddenly determined to work for with single-minded determination. The new pattern of his life was formed in that instant as he put all his untapped energies and intelligence to work.

Belton, Texas, some eight miles up the road, was the home of Baylor Female College (later Mary Hardin-Baylor) where Miriam had received her higher education. There he was able to borrow law books to read at night while he farmed during the daytime. He joined the Salado Debating Society to improve his speech and his oratorical abilities.

In 1897 he was admitted to the bar.

Now a professional man, he courted Miriam and asked her to marry him. She refused. She was twenty-two years old with limitless prospects for a much better marriage than "Farmer Jim."

Unfortunately, her life changed drastically the following year.

James Edward Ferguson

Official portrait of Governor James "Farmer Jim" Ferguson
Center for American History, UT-Austin

Miriam's father died of meningitis. The suddenness of his death left his survivors shocked and grieving. Joseph Lapshy Wallace had been a good businessman whose widow and six children—including Miriam—inherited a large estate with several thousand acres of farmland, cotton gins, stock in the Belton bank, and $50,000 in cash—a vast sum in those day.

The estate needed a manager, Mrs. Wallace decided. Who better than her distant cousin Jim Ferguson, the ambitious young lawyer whom her late husband had come to approve of? Ferguson accepted the job immediately. It was the opportunity he needed to show his worthiness to Miriam.

It also gave him access to more money than he had ever seen in his life.

In an effort to impress Miriam and to better himself socially, he ran for county attorney. Though he lost the race, he must have impressed her. Possibly her family brought pressure to bear. On the last day of the nineteenth century, they were married in her mother's parlor. Immediately he moved her to a fine new brick home in Belton, where he became a member of the Texas Bankers Association and the Farmers State Bank of Belton.

Within months their situation had improved and their status had risen. He moved her again to an even finer brick home in Temple, where he helped found the bank there. Their daughter Ouida, named for Miriam's favorite romance novelist, was born in November of 1900.

Since Jim's law practice was known to be insufficient to keep him busy, people may have wondered where the cash came from for all these banks and partnerships and fine homes. Although no one actually questioned the capital required to make all these investments, the money was undoubtedly "borrowed in Miriam's name" from Joe Wallace's estate.

Indeed, no criminality was attached to these borrowings, which in modern terms would have been considered embezzlement or at the least misappropriation of funds. In those days men were expected to protect women and to manage their business affairs. If the men lost the women's money, that was too bad, but since the women would have been presumed to do much worse, the loss was merely unfortunate and in no way felonious.

For Jim Ferguson the Bell County part of the world must have looked especially bright. The future brimmed with promise in the early years of the twentieth century. As the couple grew closer together, Miriam became convinced that Jim was, in the words of their older daughter's biography, "the most brilliant lawyer in Texas and the greatest living businessman."

A smashing success investing and spending his wife's family's money, Jim began to look around for other areas to conquer. In 1902 he entered Bell County politics as campaign manager for a local candidate's run for Congress. The candidate's loss did nothing to dampen Jim's spirit for politics. Over the next decade he moved higher and higher in the Democratic Party. In 1912 he worked on the successful campaign of O. B. Colquitt for governor. The ease with which Colquitt, the Democratic nominee, won set fire to Ferguson's ambition. He was sure his management had been instrumental in carrying that election.

Ferguson saw himself as a better choice than Colquitt. Texas needed him, he believed. With the governor of Texas encouraging him, he declared his candidacy. His speeches were masterpieces. He boasted that he knew firsthand about farming, stock raising, and business. He personalized every speech with references to his graduation from the School of Hard Knocks, something most poor people in Texas could identify with. So impressive and so sincere-sounding was he that people who heard those speeches couldn't help liking and respecting him.

His constituents from Bell County had nothing bad to say about him. They knew he had started from nothing. No one criticized him because he had married well and richly. No one commented that his wealth had grown from the capital base achieved by his wife's dead father.

On Sunday morning in 1913, Jim told his wife that he was going to run for governor. In all likelihood, he told her he was going to win. His past successes had convinced him that he was nearly invincible.

The Farm Problem

During Reconstruction when Governor A. J. Davis and his State Police foreclosed on the big plantations of East Texas, the small farmers throughout the state had not seen his actions as their problem. They had not foreseen what the absence of rich and powerful voices with many acres and many resources at their disposal would do to the economy of Texas. Within a very few years, they learned. Their small voices rising from their twenty- and forty-acre plots made no impression on the powerful corporations that grew into monopolies as the century turned.

The Farmer's Alliance, which later became the great third party movement of Populism, began in Lampasas, Texas, in 1875. The "dirt farmers," the backbone of the country, were earning almost no money working alone on their small farms. A half bale of cotton per acre was considered a splendid crop. Without the farmer's children to pick it, it wouldn't have been worth planting. From the oldest sons and daughters down to the two- and three-year-old toddlers, they worked as unpaid laborers from dawn to dusk.

Texas farmers as well as farmers everywhere had reason to believe that the best land had been taken by the law of eminent domain for the railroads. In addition to taking the land, the railroads constituted a monopoly that charged the farmer more than a fair cost for hauling his produce to market. Robber barons Jay Gould and his contemporaries crisscrossed the country making enormous profits in hauling fees from thousands of people they served.

Ironically, neither the railroads nor the eastern corporations were more than marginally at fault. Though their rates seemed exorbitant, they were recouping the tremendous outlays of railroad construction.

The real problem for the farmer was that farming was and is to this day cyclical. Prices for products fluctuate with demand, often affected by markets thousands of miles away. These fluctuations are particularly evident in the case of cotton, which—unlike perishable foodstuffs—can be stored for years.

The small farmer could no longer earn a living by the sweat of his brow because he needed immediate return at the end of each growing season in order to survive. Even when he received it, prices based on supply and demand in some years kept him from making enough money to pay his debts. Even the local politicians, ignorant of European markets and U.S. tariffs, did not truly understand his problems.

Nothing had been done since 1888 when the Texas Democratic Party recognized the plight of the farmer by adding anti-trust legislation and railroad regulation to their "wish" lists. Legislation and regulation are worse than nothing if they sit stalled on the "back burner" in politics. They allow politicians to make speeches telling their supporters that they have "fought for them" when actually they have done nothing concrete.

The strongest fear among these farmers was that their places, small though they were, would be lost to Negroes and others they considered as undesirables. In response to these fears the Texas Legislature levied a poll tax as a requirement for voting. As a tax it was nearly foolproof for a politician. It cost him nothing to pass it in terms of his own re-election. It brought some money into the public coffers. And it effectively decreased the voting base, making him responsible to a fewer number of people. It disenfranchised the poorest and therefore the least empowered citizens of the state who could not be counted on to contribute to his campaign for re-election.

Then in 1900 the cycle of poor farm prices turned. The North required more products as it became more urbanized. European markets strengthened as France and Germany took a breather from their hostilities. The Texas farmer's plight miraculously eased.

Again the politicians were miraculously saved. The voter did not realize his feeble local legislation had had almost no effect. He certainly did not realize that he had become a mere wheel in an increasingly complex piece of machinery that would bind American regions together and end isolation from Europe forever.

Never more clearly was this phenomenon shown than in 1914. Europe was plunged into World War I. Cotton and cattle prices plummeted.

The time of great trouble across the country gave rise to a prohibition movement. In the minds of many Americans, they must have been doing something wrong. Otherwise, things would have been better. Or so preached the fundamentalist ministers who moved to the small towns and hamlets across Texas. There they found tiny desperate congregations willing to listen to their Bible-thumping condemnations. Somehow, drinking alcohol became mixed with sin and the evils besetting America at that time.

In Texas where all was confusion and disarray, farmers and ranchers needed a voice as never before.

Farmer Jim

James Edward Ferguson had almost no understanding of tariffs and European markets. While he was supremely ambitious, he lacked the education to formulate a program that would improve anyone's lot. He had no notion of how to attack the economic and political causes of the farmers' problems.

But while he had no political mission, he had a personal one—to be the governor of Texas so that Miriam Wallace would never believe she had married beneath herself. He therefore selected his campaign issues by the number of votes they would garner.

Himself a banker and a deep conservative with a considerable fortune in stocks and bonds in his care, he began his campaign as the rich man's candidate. He shied away from the prohibition issue, since those who were wealthy and sophisticated attended organized Methodist and Episcopalian churches among whose congregations social drinking was merely frowned upon rather than actually condemned.

With these stances he gained the attention of the newspapers in the cities. He also proved himself to be unequaled as a political speaker.

When he took his campaign to the countryside, he made 145 speeches in the Cotton Belt alone, only ten of which were in the cities. He knew exactly what he was doing. The years 1913-1914 saw a national depression. Hundreds of ranchers and thousands of farmers went bankrupt. Especially tragic was the fact that two-thirds of the Texas cotton crop, valued at $210 million in 1910, was exported to Europe. This most valuable export among all United States exports was largely responsible for maintaining the favorable balance of trade.

How could cotton be worth so much money when more than half of the men who grew it had seen their proud independence swept away? Half the farmers in Texas had become sharecroppers. Fifty years of price cycles and corporate greed had created a vast mass of American peasants akin to those in Europe.

However, they were peasants with a difference. In response to Jim Ferguson's eloquence, each and every one was willing to plunk down $2.75 for a poll tax receipt to vote for him. They saw him as the man who understood them—he was the man to elect. In today's money the poll tax would probably amount to $300 or $400 yearly.

How many people would be willing to pay such a sum today for the right to vote?

The year 1914 saw the beginning of "Fergusonism," a political philosophy loosely described as "a freewheeling, loose-scrupled boondocks liberalism." From 1914 through 1935 one political watcher commented: "With old Jim, you were either for 'im or agin' 'im. There wasn't any middle of the road."

The first and most important plank in Ferguson's platform—when it was finally devised—was like a stake through the heart of the deeply conservative landowners of Texas. Many of these men had managed to acquire vast acreages, one twenty-acre plot at a time. They wanted the status quo because for them it worked admirably. Without suffering, they were able to make money from the backbreaking labor of others.

Moreover, they wanted no social programs to aid the poor. They saw no need for them. If the farmer could not pay his taxes, they would foreclose on his land but allow him to stay and farm it for them. If he still could not make a living, he and his family were to be pitied as they were evicted, but there were others waiting for the opportunity to try.

Jim Ferguson promised to regulate tenant farming. Ordinarily, sharecroppers paid their landlord one-fourth of the profits from their cotton crops and one-third from the other crops. As good land became scarcer, greedy landlords demanded bonuses of so much per bale or bushel in addition to the quarter-rents if the crops were good. It was a disincentive to producing a good crop besides cheating the farmer of his fair share of the profit.

By promising to "fix rents" as state law, "Farmer Jim" galvanized the farmers against the other Democratic candidate, Thomas H. Ball, a Houston lawyer (unpopular then as now). Ferguson won the nomination by 50,000 votes and the election by 150,000.

He took office in January 1915. True to his promise, Ferguson induced the Texas Congress to pass a bill against the bonuses. Even though the landlords carried the law to the Supreme Court where it was subsequently declared unconstitutional, Ferguson enshrined himself in the hearts and minds of ordinary Texas voters.

Forgetting that his own pitiful elementary education had been as a result of his bad behavior, Ferguson became the "Education Governor." He signed a bill for state aid to rural schools and another for compulsory school attendance. In its own way this bill was revolutionary in an agricultural state. Farmers could not work their children as farmhands for 365 days a year. All working people had to keep their children in school until age sixteen. No one had a choice not to be educated.

Three new normal schools for the instruction of teachers were authorized. The Austin State School was established, and other eleemosynary institutions for handicapped children were provided for. Colleges were funded to begin building programs, and educational appropriation bills were passed.

To provide the money for these educational improvements, the ad valorem taxes rose from 12½ cents to 30 cents per $100 valuation of property and products. The rise in tax rates was the first fly in the ointment of Ferguson's administration. Then as now a tax bill at the end of an administration leaves people with a bad taste in their mouths.

Nevertheless, Jim and Miriam went to the Democratic National Convention in St. Louis in 1916. From the platform, the Texas governor made an impassioned speech against woman suffrage. Fortunately, the suffrage plank passed by a large majority. Ironically, he would have cause to give thanks for its passage.

Back in Austin in 1916 his second campaign did not go as smoothly as his first had done. The ad valorem tax was uppermost in men's minds. He was under attack from all sides. His opponents brought forth the evidence that Ferguson had appropriated state funds for his own use, had deposited state funds in a bank in which he owned stock, and had accepted but never repaid a campaign loan of $156,000 from an unknown source.

The evidence overwhelmed his popularity because Ferguson had run through all kinds of funds, as well as Miriam's inheritance, to a shocking degree. The poor who were his greatest supporters began to take note of the way he lived. His opponents started rumors that Miriam and Jim never wore the same clothes twice. Once they took them off, they were believed to dump them down a chute. Women wrote to Miriam asking her to send them her clothes rather than throw them away.

Well known across Texas was that Ferguson had found a way to supplement the $4,000 income that the governorship of Texas paid per year. He began to issue pardons to criminals—in particular those whose lawyers made contributions to his campaign.

Ferguson was re-elected in November 1916, but by only 60,000 votes. Against a Republican candidate, whose party had been anathema since the Civil War, the margin should have been much greater.

At the beginning of his term, the highway department was instituted and the ad valorem tax was raised again to the top rate allowed by the Texas Constitution—35 cents. More and more people disliked him, and fewer and fewer defended him when he quarreled with the Board of Regents of the University of Texas.

Calling the faculty members "butterfly chasers," he sought to force the regents to fire several professors. They refused. On June 2 he vetoed the 1.6 million dollar appropriation with the lame excuse that the amount was excessive. Immediately, Ferguson found himself in trouble.

The University of Texas was a formidable institution, graduating most of the best minds in the state including many Texas congressmen as well as most members of the courts. Its alumni did not take kindly to the upstart with no degree whatsoever judging professors with several. On July 21 he was called to appear before the Travis County Grand Jury where he was indicted on nine charges, foremost of which was misappropriation of funds.

He would have gone to jail had he not made bond of $13,000.

Where or from whom the money came no one knew for sure, but many would speculate endlessly. The Texas Legislature was called back to Austin to sit in special session. Three weeks later—during which time Ferguson announced that he would run for an unprecedented third term as governor—the representatives prepared twenty-one articles of impeachment.

The State Senate sat for three more weeks before convicting Ferguson on ten of the articles. One of only three men to vote against the governor's impeachment was the senator from Duval County, Archer Parr, who remained Ferguson's steadfast friend and cohort.

Ferguson was charged on five counts of misappropriation of public funds, three related to his conduct in regard to the University of Texas, one for failing to enforce banking laws, and one for contempt for refusing to reveal where and why he acquired $156,000 during his first term.

As quickly as possible some said, "with his tail between his legs," Jim Ferguson took his family back to Temple.

The truth was that he never gave up. While Miriam and daughters Ouida and Dorrace tried to regain some measure of their old prestige in the community, their husband and father fought as never before.

He started a weekly newspaper—*The Ferguson Forum*—which the Prohibitionists referred to snidely as *Ferguson For Rum*. He sued several big daily newspapers in Texas for libel. As World War I threatened to extend its battles across the ocean to America, conservative editors accused him of getting the $156,000 from the German Kaiser as bribery to commit acts of treason in Texas. Seething with righteous indignation, he won his suit against three major papers. The settlement was substantial enough to allow the *Forum* to circulate statewide. As has already been stated, people were either "for 'im or agin' 'im."

Through the *Forum* he was able to keep his name in front of the people of Texas, who soon forgot the particulars of his impeachment and only knew they liked what they read. For the next twenty years Fergusonism dominated the state's political thought.

Still, the entire state looked on in amazement as he ran again for governor in 1918. His candidacy was illegal, and William P. Hobby was overwhelmingly elected. Yet the "Never say Die, say Damn!" motto that he had adopted for the family stirred Texan's minds and hearts.

Barred from running for governor of Texas again, in 1920 he ran as an unsuccessful candidate for president on the American (Know Nothing) Party, a direct descendant of the Farmer's Alliance, which had become the Populist Party in the previous century. In 1922 he was an unsuccessful candidate for U.S. senator.

James Edward Ferguson

Opposition to him ran high before and after his impeachment.
Note the accusation of German Kaiser sympathies on the sign.
He won his suit for slander on this issue.
Center for American History, UT-Austin

Hardheaded as a mule, he was finally forced to accept as fact that he could not win an office in the state of Texas. Then brash, bold, never-say-die Farmer Jim proposed the most revolutionary candidate in the history of the United States.

In 1924 he proposed Miriam Wallace Ferguson to run against Judge Felix Robertson of Dallas, the candidate of the Ku Klux Klan.

History's Assessment

Political manipulator par excellence though he might have been, James Edward Ferguson's greed for the things money could buy undoubtedly brought about his downfall. Poor as only a circuit-riding minister's son can be, when he married Miriam Wallace, he luxuriated in her wealth. At first everything went well, but as he saw his investments slipping away, he used his political skills to regain them.

To his credit he did not forget the people who voted for him. Rural schools were championed as never before. He sought and won for a short time a fixed rent for the tenant farmers. No wonder they voted for him. When his wife ran in 1924, their wives did too.

Perhaps he was not so far wrong in his own grandiose statement on his first two years: "All told, it is generally admitted that my first administration was one of the most successful in the state's history."

"The Sunbonnet Governor"

Miriam Amanda Wallace Ferguson

"I am interested only in making history."

Running For Election

When the Ferguson family and the Democratic Party decided to run Miriam Ferguson in the place of her impeached husband, they latched onto an image that they calculated would appeal to the majority of Texas voters—the "domestic" woman.

The idea to run her in the first place came from her husband "Farmer Jim." As politically savvy as the former governor was, he had seized her candidacy as his way to return to power when by Texas law he could not hold state office again since he had been impeached. He realized he could utilize the woman suffrage amendment, which he had opposed in 1916, in as daring a move as any politician has ever made.

In her book *The Fergusons of Texas or Two Governors for the Price of One*, their daughter Ouida Ferguson Nalle tells how she rushed over from Austin to tell Jim that the court had handed down its decision barring his name from the gubernatorial ticket forever. She burst into her father's hotel room in Taylor, Texas, where he had just finished making a speech.

A dynamic and passionate speaker, he had removed his coat and now sat on the edge of the bed to cool off. In his sweat-stained shirt, he looked less like a politician and more like the farmer that he claimed to be. When Ouida finished her tale of woe, he looked up calmly.

"What are you going to do now?" Ouida asked sympathetically.

Without hesitation came the answer. "Your mother can run."

Though Ouida does not mention his expression, he must have grinned. Perhaps he gave a sly wink, for he had found another way to put one over. Expecting the worst from the state he had once governed, he had already filed Miriam's name.

Woman suffrage, the Nineteenth Amendment to the Constitution adopted August 26, 1920, was a new thing. Most Texas women hadn't even considered voting, much less running for office. Only four years later, a female candidate was running for the highest office in the state. Those who were devoutly against females voting must have raised a great hue and cry.

Mostly, no one took Jim's wife's candidacy seriously at first. Newspapers across Texas beginning with the *Houston Press* carried the story as a sort of novelty.

Women weren't suited to public office. Everyone knew that. But no one could fault her when as Miriam Amanda Wallace Ferguson herself wrote in 1922 in the *Ferguson Forum*, "I never fought for woman suffrage, but they made it law, they gave us the ballot, and I see no reason why we should not exercise our right."

Her candidacy was treated by her opponents as what it was—a circumvention by Jim Ferguson to regain the governorship.

When her picture appeared in the newspapers, the caption beneath her name was M. A. Ferguson, exactly as it would have

Miriam Amanda Wallace Ferguson

Miriam Amanda Wallace as Jim first saw her. Born to wealth and privilege, better educated than most women of her time, she was not interested in him. *Center for American History, UT-Austin*

been for a man at that time. Immediately the press nicknamed her "Ma" or "Maw" when they added the initial for her maiden name.

For a woman who had been born to wealth and property as well as a respected place in Bell County society, the name was demeaning and insulting. The newspapers, written by men in large part for the perusal of men, meant it to be so. They took great pleasure in pointing out that her only previous interest in adding to the general welfare of the state had been to order a greenhouse to be built onto a corner of the governor's mansion. There she cultivated the flowers with which she decorated the house.

She wasn't a serious candidate.

Her opponents thought so too. Several candidates including Felix Robertson of Dallas, the office-seeker for the Ku Klux Klan, made fun of her at the same time they reminded voters of her husband's impeachment. No right-minded Texan should vote for her.

But a new campaign blossomed among the farmers, who remembered all that "Farmer Jim" had done for rural education of their children. Across the state the first bumper-sticker campaign began. "Me for Ma!" And on full-blown signs were added the words, "And I Ain't Got a Dern Thing Against Pa."

Both Fergusons knew where their strengths lay. On the campaign trail they would gauge their audiences. If the voters were German farmers from Fredericksburg, Ma would introduce herself or—more often—allow someone else to do so. She would survey the audience with thin-lipped solemnity.

(Though she was a cheerful woman, she was said never to have allowed herself to smile. She felt that a serious expression was essential to her image of a woman not just running for the highest elective office in the state but one whose husband had been wronged.)

Miriam Amanda Wallace Ferguson

After brief opening remarks in which she called upon the mothers, sisters, and wives of Texas to help her clear her family's name, she would speak about her children and her grandson, whom she sometimes had on the platform with her. She would tell them how she wanted the little boy to be able to say, "As a rebuke to the impeachment that denied my grandfather the right to go to the people, my dear grandmother was elected governor by the people of Texas—the first woman governor in the world."

Then she would announce with eyes properly downcast, "My husband will make the speech."

Ma and Farmer Jim knew that every German farmer to a man was uneasy if not downright opposed to woman suffrage. Not a single vote would go for Ma if they believed she was going to "wear the pants in the family."

In that vein Jim would light into his opponents and the Ku Klux Klan with all the oratorical power of which he was capable. Sometime during his speech "for Ma," he would draw a laugh and a round of applause when he'd say something like, "If those women want to suffer, I say let 'em suffer." Sometimes he would even go so far as to mention the speech he had made at the 1916 Democratic National Convention in which he deplored the Women's Movement and urged against giving them the vote.

He did not mention that if the amendment had not passed, he would never have been able to run his wife for governor. Whether many in the crowd appreciated the irony of the situation is unknown.

In front of more sophisticated crowds, when people yelled that she was going to do exactly what her husband told her to do, she declared that, of course, she would rely on her husband's experience. Why should she not? And lucky Texas voters would get twice as much for their votes—"two governors for the price of one."

The planks in her platform were negligible. Other than erroneously promising the state of Texas the honor of electing the "first woman governor in the world," she promised to vindicate her husband's actions and clear his name. And most important, she was an avowed enemy of the Ku Klux Klan, a powerful and frightening force in Texas politics in 1924. Felix Robertson stood for the God-given right and supremacy of white Christian men. Overtly or secretly, many "white Christian men" agreed with him.

The Klan held a strong appeal to Texans who remembered the atrocious outlawry of E. J. Davis's regime when the State Guards and Military Reserves could declare martial law in any county in Texas and force the citizens living in it to pay the expenses of the occupation forces. Robertson's oratory constantly informed his audiences that the State Guards had been made up almost entirely of criminals, crazy persons, and Negroes.

To the credit of Texas and Texans, the Klan was not and never had been the voice of the majority of the electorate. By 1924 the organization had hidden themselves "behind the mask" too long. They were no longer the Knights of the White Magnolia that General Nathan Bedford Forrest organized to control the black vote being utilized en masse by Radical Republican Reconstructionists. Instead, criminals and paranoids of the type that once flocked to E. J. Davis's State Guards had infiltrated the ranks of the twentieth-century Klan.

Moreover, part of the focus of the Klan attack was absent in Texas. While World War I had made the eastern shores of the nation aware that many of their numbers were so-called hyphenated Americans, not many real foreigners lived in Texas. The German farmers of central Texas, the Irish farmers in San Patricio County, and the Mexican ranchers of South Texas all had family ties dating back before 1836. They had been Texans long before they became Americans.

The state was remarkably clear of religious prejudice. When the Klan spouted anti-Semitism, where almost no one was Jewish, and anti-Catholicism against the Hispanic population that was in most cases more Texan than the Anglo Texans, most citizens turned deaf ears.

Its most obvious target, however, was a group that many Texans considered unworthy of citizenship—the Negroes, who were having little success in assimilating into the population.

In short the Klan had become a white supremacist movement that had gone ethnocentric, Protestant, and above all secretive. It operated as a vigilante organization pretending to uphold the morals of the state. As such it acted as prosecutor, judge, and jury against supposed criminals, loose women, and uppity "niggers." It also persecuted anyone in the community who might speak to reason by condemning its actions. Like any other secret organization, its power had been corrupted by members who used it to carry out personal vendettas.

It was also dangerous. Its members were responsible for dozens of documented vicious, violent attacks against anyone who opposed them. Many law officers in rural communities across the state joined the group rather than risk being singled out by some disgruntled member with a grudge. Unfortunately, their presence lent legitimacy to all sorts of abuses.

Galloping around the countryside on horseback, setting fires, dragging people out of their beds and into the woods for beatings and floggings, they were a bane on the countryside.

And Texas listened when Ma Ferguson stood up and spoke against them. It was the issue she and Pa needed. She was the candidate the Klan feared. She was the candidate that they could have no argument against—white, Protestant, a wife and mother, and a thoroughly good woman. Who could argue with her credentials?

As if to emphasize its own disgraceful behavior, on July 26, the day of the primary election, the white-sheeted crew threw rocks at the Fergusons' home in Temple.

The attack backfired.

The stoning of a woman's house and the trespass upon her property were duly reported in the newspapers. Texas men in general regarded a war on such a woman as the act of animals rather than men.

In later speeches Ma and Pa made fun of their "feeble" attacks against a righteous family and democracy in general. The attacks had actually been a blessing for the Ferguson campaign. People and in particular women who had never voted came out and cast their votes in sympathy. In a race with nine candidates, Ma came in second behind Felix Robertson. She was in the runoff.

When reporters came to Ma's house the next day to hear her reaction to her first step on the road to victory, she wasn't pleased with their intrusion. The Klan had shown her what she had lost in terms of civility. The press showed her what she would lose in terms of privacy.

She had planned to make peach preserves that day. Ouida, more like "Farmer Jim" than anyone suspected, suggested that her mother let the photographers take pictures of her in her kitchen peeling peaches.

The press was delighted, taking pictures, noting her recipe to print in the papers, tasting the results. If they knew she resented their presence, they never wrote about it. Later they accompanied her out to her father's Bell County farm where she had been born.

Though Ma was appalled at the idea, Ouida posed her wearing a sunbonnet, the traditional headgear a Texas farm woman used to protect her complexion from the ravages of sun and wind. It was a big floppy wide-brimmed piece of gingham or calico with lappets hanging down the back of the neck. It had been fashioned after a Victorian duster cap. The reporters must have felt they were writing stories about their grandmother.

The one Ouida borrowed from one of the women who actually worked on the Wallace farm was soiled. When Ma protested, her daughter turned it inside out, dimming the printed calico to a speckled gray.

So a campaign song was adopted almost immediately. "Put on Your Old Gray Bonnet" was played to Ma's annoyance throughout her many, many public appearances thereafter. Privately she hated the entire idea. She was sure that she was making a fool of herself posing in a garment she wouldn't be caught dead in. Still, the newspapers were selling her story across the state. She was getting more print space than any other candidate.

Even so, the Fergusons needed every vote, and to get them the sacrifices had to go on and on. Ma had lost civility. She had lost privacy. She had demeaned herself. By Election Day she would wince visibly every time the band swung into "Put on Your Old Gray Bonnet." But the worst was yet to come.

Had she known what she would have to do when her husband proposed her name, would she have run?

We will never know.

Close to one hundred days stood between the Fergusons and election. In those days Texas was the biggest state in the union by far—an expanse of more than a quarter million square miles (over 100,000 more than California). The Fergusons were forced to spread themselves thin to cover more ground. Ma and Pa had to take separate campaign trails.

The result was that Ma had to make her own speeches.

She would surprise even herself. She had never made a public speech before her announcement to run for governor. Now she was called upon to make them daily, standing on the platforms, staring at the seas of strange faces alone. Since it is a well-known fact that thousands of people fear public speaking more than death itself, what hidden depths of courage and self-possession she must have tapped.

Rising to the occasion to tell the voters what great wrongs had been done to her husband and to vilify the masked and robed outlaws, she made impassioned speeches most effective because they were honest from her point of view. Voters loved her. And more and more among them came to despise the Klan.

On his campaign trail, Robertson was frequently called to answer for the Klan's attack. Since he had no civil answer, that single incident undoubtedly cost him many votes.

Texas was ready for Ma Ferguson. They liked the idea of electing the first woman governor. Moreover, the Klan had become as much an embarrassment for their white sheets and peaked hoods as for their radical philosophies. The small world of Texas politics was extending beyond the county and the state. U.S. representatives and senators with such views were not accorded much respect among their liberal northern fellows.

One newspaper paraphrased Henry Holcomb Bennett's poem "The Flag Goes By" with

> Hoods off!
> Along the street there comes
> Patriotic daughters and loyal sons,
> A crowd of bonnets beneath the sky,
> Hoods off!
> Miriam Ferguson is passing by.

Compromise and concession were not in the Klan vocabulary. Fearful of their declining power, their attacks were becoming more violent and more widespread. White-hooded horsemen galloped through the East Texas forests. Gangs of white-robed figures climbed into the backs of pickups and rattled off along backcountry roads. In their effort of stop Ma's landslide, recently enfranchised women and Hispanics became their targets. A groundswell of public opinion arose against them.

In the run-off primary, Ma trounced the Ku Klux Klan candidate by 98,000 votes. It was a miracle. A woman had actually beaten a man.

Still the family remained cautious. Her Republican opponent, Dr. George Butte, was a professor at the University of Texas. University graduates could be counted on not to forget Jim's veto of the $1.6 million appropriation for the institution. Unfortunately for Butte, the liberals and the Klan threw their support behind him. Their presence was the worst thing that could have happened to him. Besides being from the "wrong" party, he now had crazies on his side.

Ma and Pa hit the campaign trail again and did not stop until her victory in the general election. In the end Butte could not overcome his own supporters. Ma beat him by 125,000 votes.

Former Governor William Hobby, newly appointed head of the *Houston Post*, editorialized, "Many will vote for Ma Ferguson, but no one will vote for her because he thinks she is more capable than Dr. Butte."

Her election was a worldwide sensation. Europeans were amazed at her ascendancy. They had had queens sitting on their thrones by right of inheritance, but no country had actually elected a woman to a leadership position.

In truth Miriam Ferguson was the first woman *elected* to an executive position in the entire world. As a footnote to history, little if any attention was paid to the fact that Ferguson would be inaugurated fifteen days *after* Nellie Tayloe Ross of Wyoming, making her the second woman governor in the U.S. Nellie's majority was not the overwhelming numbers that Miriam garnered. The state had qualified for statehood by doubling its electorate to include women before the U.S. Constitutional amendment granted it to all women in 1920. To this day it remains one of the least populous states in America.

Big, bold, boastful Texas had captured the imagination of America and the world. For all women everywhere a new day had dawned.

Governing the State

If Texas voters expected Miriam Wallace Ferguson to attend her own inauguration in an old gray bonnet, they were badly disappointed. Her folksiness disappeared like a cast-off cloak. Likewise, she abandoned the more retiring "wife of the governor" image with which she had appeared at Jim's side in 1915.

Like a queen she dressed in a black satin dress with a chinchilla collar. Over the fur she added a deep ivory feather boa. While the band played "Texas, Our Texas," one can almost see her flinging one of the ends back over her shoulder as she straightened her back, lifted her chin, and thinned her mouth into her characteristic firm, sober line.

How those lips must have quivered as—beneath the crossed sabers of the Sul Ross Volunteers from Texas A&M University—she marched into her inauguration! What secret elation! What secret fears were rushing through her brain? She could not have helped but feel excitement and pride. She could not have helped but feel what had been entrusted to her.

At the beginning of the run, when her husband had announced his intentions for her, she could not have believed that she would ever achieve the seat she now ascended to. She must have applauded herself, knowing how hard she had worked to attain it. Given her spotless reputation and sense of responsibility, promises she had made over and over in countless speeches must have been uppermost in her mind.

Was one sentence repeating itself? "I am not seeking glory but only trying to lift a burden that is hard to bear."

She had three inaugural balls that night. One was held in the Senate Chamber, the second in the Austin Hotel, and the third in the venerable Driskill Hotel built in 1886. Dressed in a heavily beaded, flesh-pink silk chiffon for the celebrations, she represented a new era in politics and certainly a new kind of governor. No one alive today except perhaps Ann Richards, who stepped into her shoes three-quarters of century later, can truly appreciate what she faced as a woman governor in a male-dominated state.

Her daughter wrote of their return. "All of us piled into the old twin-six Packard, with Mamma at the wheel. It was the very same car in which we had departed from the Governor's Mansion in 1917. As Mamma pulled up the hand brake under the old porte cochere at the mansion, the new governor of Texas said, as if addressing the old chariot: 'Well, we have returned! We departed in disgrace; we now return in glory!'"

Two days later she discovered her name had been chiseled out of the cement block at the entrance to her beloved greenhouse. In a burst of anger, she sent immediately for workmen to restore it along with the 1915 date.

During the forties one of the governors was asked why he didn't have it taken out. He replied that he didn't dare. He might make Ma so mad "she'd run again."

According to their secretaries, the Fergusons went to work every day at nine o'clock. They worked side by side at separate desks until Ma retired at three. Farmer Jim stayed on until five. Promptly at six, dinner was served in the executive mansion dining room after which the couple read or wrote until bedtime.

Ma's first act was to fight the legislature for a massive cut in the state budget, as she and every politician since time immemorial has promised to do. In this case she was successful. After the battle she was able to reduce it by thirteen million, a substantial amount in a state where many people earned a dollar a day.

With great pleasure and a great deal of publicity, she signed an anti-mask bill. It was a deathblow to the Ku Klux Klan. Probably half its membership had been more or less coerced into joining. Now they could be arrested for wearing their hoods. The undedicated melted away. Out of favor with both Democrats and Republicans, despised by the majority of the people of Texas, they simply disappeared, melted back into the darkness from which they had emerged. Their dissolution was Ma's crowning achievement.

Her popularity did not last long, however. On April 4, 1925, she signed an amnesty bill restoring James Edward Ferguson's right to hold office in Texas. The newspapers cried foul, and many voters were disenchanted.

Other problems beset them as well. The Fergusons were no longer wealthy. Jim had spent most of the money Miriam had inherited from her father. The governor of Texas was still paid only $4,000 per annum. The executive secretary received $3,000. Also on staff were a bookkeeper, a personal secretary, and a file clerk. The entire executive branch of the state consisted of five paid employees and the governor's husband.

Again the practice of issuing pardons began. Nola Wood, the personal secretary to both Jim and Miriam, insisted that Ma "didn't know a thing about being governor" but she loved doing "good." Issuing pardons was doing "good." Nola, who was in charge of writing out all the pardons, remembers gifts of cold cash rolled in newspapers and handed to Jim by "big boys" who got paroles from him. She remembers taking small amounts such as $400 and huge amounts like $10,000 back to the vault in the Governor's Mansion.

The amounts were always in cash because no record was kept of cash money brought into or going out of the office.

Later Nola Wood's story was discounted by Ghent Sanderford, who served as Ma's executive secretary. However, the unimaginable number of pardons that bore Ma's signature leaves the historian to believe that illegality was rampant. Furthermore, Ma had to have known what she was doing, since she and Pa shared the same office.

She is known to have issued 1,161 pardons in two years. Indeed, T. R. Fehrenbach, in his history *Lone Star: A History of Texas and the Texans*, puts the number much higher: 2,000 convicts either pardoned, furloughed, or otherwise freed in twenty months. Some individuals did not even reach the penitentiary but were paroled as soon as their trial was over.

Pa Ferguson is reported to have asked her, "Shouldn't you find out what they did before you pardon them, Miriam?"

When approached about the excessive liberality of her policies, Ma attributed it to Pa's anti-Prohibitionist stance. She explained that the penitentiaries were filled with bootleggers who she believed were not really violent or dangerous men. She felt they should be home taking care of their wives and children and saving the taxpayer unwanted burdens.

In contradiction of her statement is the known fact that during the last weeks of her administration, she freed 33 rapists, 124 robbers, 127 liquor violators, and 133 murderers. Nights when there was an electrocution in the penitentiary at Huntsville, the warden called to be sure that Miriam was not going to commute the sentence. When she didn't, she usually hung up the receiver and burst into tears.

The release of over 400 felons, many of whom were deadly dangerous to the citizens of the state, must have done much to lower the morale of the Texas Rangers and other law enforcement units after all the hard and dangerous work of bringing them in. Likewise, the courts must have been furious after the expense of bringing all these people to trial and convicting them. To have them summarily released to prey again on the countryside was a national disgrace.

Whether any of this was pointed out to the Fergusons is unknown. It seems unlikely that they could have pardoned so many without more than one irate dispenser of justice storming into their office and having his say.

Besides the pardons, Jim Ferguson was known to be awarding highway and railroad right-of-way contracts to cronies. Texas Attorney General Dan Moody launched an investigation that put the Fergusons on the defensive. While no indictments were ever handed down and no money was ever traced to the Governor's Mansion, Moody's publicity was enough.

In 1926 Ma lost the election to her attorney general by 200,000 votes. In response she did what the twenty-first century has come to call "playing the sex card." She accused the people of Texas of not allowing her the traditional second term they generally gave to all male governors.

However, people in Texas knew what they knew. When the Fergusons were able to build a Spanish Colonial home on Windsor Road in Austin and buy a cattle ranch in Bosque County, even her most ardent supporters concluded that something had happened in the Governor's Mansion that had increased the Ferguson fortunes remarkably.

When Jim tried to run for office in 1930, the Democratic Executive Committee refused to certify him. To make certain, the Texas Supreme Court declared the Amnesty Bill unconstitutional.

Ma would have to run again. Her 1930 campaign was of special interest to many of Jim's supporters, in particular to lawyer Jim Wells of Cameron County and state senator Archie Parr, the "Duke of Duval." In a freebooter state like Texas, people were again ready for a change—and Wells and Parr set about to give it to them.

Governor Dan Moody, who had served for three terms, commanded that formidable force the Texas Rangers. Moody was moreover as tough on crime as Ma was lenient. His administration had harassed the forces of corruption constantly.

Ma received the most votes in the Democratic primary but lost the runoff to Ross Sterling, a past president of Humble Oil, the self-described "Big Fat Boy from Buffalo Bayou." The demographics of the state were changing rapidly. The cities voted overwhelming for the "big oil" candidate.

Sterling was the "businessmen's candidate," an ultra-conservative who held out the hope of putting Texas back on the road to prosperity. The rest of the United States had plunged into the depths of a depression that had men jumping out of windows on Wall Street and riding the rails between hobo jungles all across the country.

Sterling never really had a chance to show what his business expertise could do. Farm prices, mineral production, and attempts at industrialization all staggered under crippling losses. Taxes became uncollectible. The governor had to veto measure after measure because there was no money to pay to implement it.

Sterling also was forced to declare martial law in the East Texas oil field. Ma and Pa had themselves an issue that gained strength when the *Houston Post* revealed that Humble had advanced Sterling a $175,000 bonus on a lease and $250,000 in deferred royalties right before his election campaign in 1930.

Such funds made Jim Ferguson's $156,000, which was now known to have come from the Texas Brewers' Association, look like small potatoes.

In 1932 the rural voters, always strong supporters of the Fergusons and organized by such county leaders as Wells and Parr, won the race but not by a clear majority. The number of people in rural areas had declined while the urban areas were growing fast. Miriam won the first primary by 110,000 and then the runoff by not quite 4,000 votes out of almost a million cast.

To ensure her election, the Duval and Cameron County boys were at work as well as other bosses across the state. Governor Sterling's supporters protested the vote and asked for time to investigate the one hundred pro-Ferguson counties where the votes cast outnumbered the poll tax receipts. Still, the Democratic State Convention in Lubbock declared Ma the winner. Back in Austin, Sterling's forces got a judge to issue a citation for an injunction to keep Ma's name off the ballot in November. The citation had to be served by midnight.

Jim and Ma were hiding out in Ouida's house in Austin. A policeman came to the door to serve the papers, but Ouida turned him away. A few minutes later a friend came to warn them that the officer was coming back with help to search the house.

In complete darkness the family fled down the back stairs. Ouida's husband, George Nalle, backed the car out of the garage. They all climbed in, and he drove at top speed for their Bosque County ranch. Not until they crossed the county line did they all breathe a sigh of relief. Later when the story was told, Texans all across the state laughed.

Texas has always loved her outlaws.

At her second set of inaugural balls, eight years after the first, Ma suggested square dancing. The Great Depression was at its worst. Franklin Delano Roosevelt had just been elected, and Ma and Pa had to implement his reform program.

Her first efforts were to control the problem of "runaway" oil (which will be discussed later in this book). Sterling's big oil interests had been particularly against this issue, but Ma succeeded in getting the legislature to pass a two-cents-per-barrel tax on the state's oil production, the first step toward regulation and conservation of the state's most important natural resource.

With that money coming in, Ma insisted that the legislature adopt a constitutional amendment allowing the state to issue twenty million dollars in "bread bonds" for relief of the destitute. Of all that can be said against Ma, she truly sympathized with the plight of families in need.

Miriam Amanda Wallace Ferguson

Ma and Pa Ferguson remained powerful influences in Texas even after Ma's defeat by Ross Sterling in 1932. *Center for American History, UT-Austin*

Her other decisive order during her second administration began as follows: "I, Governor Miriam Ferguson, by virtue of the authority assumed by me, do hereby order all the banks in the state of Texas closed indefinitely." March 2 was Texas Independence Day, a bank holiday. She ordered that all the banks remain closed on March 3. Thus she was a step ahead of Roosevelt, who issued a national order three days later that prevented a run on the banks nationwide. By preempting the president, she was credited with saving the economy of Texas.

Important business out of the way, she went back to her old standby—pardoning convicts wholesale. Undoubtedly the Fergusons collected money in the process. Her enemies referred to the Executive Building as "the House of a Thousand Pardons."

When she left office, she swore she would never run again. Like an old fire horse that hears the bell, she was called to run in 1940, but she lost to the Lightcrust Doughboy Band of W. Lee (Pappy) O'Daniel. The day of the platform speech was being superceded by the radio. O'Daniel, a flour salesman, could buy the time. His platform was the Ten Commandments and his theme song "Pass the Biscuits, Pappy" made everybody happy. Moreover, the percentage of farmers in the United States had declined from 42 percent at the beginning of the century to just 23 percent in 1940.

"The Old Gray Bonnet" lost badly. But Ma and Pa were still a political power to be reckoned with, and everyone in the state of Texas knew it.

In 1941 a new figure appeared in the Fergusons' political circle—young Congressman Lyndon Baines Johnson, who had been defeated in his race for the U.S. Senate by Pappy O'Daniel.

At this point the motives become so tangled as to seem devised in a Theater of the Absurd. The Fergusons had backed O'Daniel, even though he had defeated Ma in her race for governor. The reason for their support was not because they liked O'Daniel, but because their friend Coke Stevenson wanted to be governor. Though Johnson led O'Daniel in the primary, Ferguson called out election chairmen in the rural counties. Amazingly the votes were "corrected" to push O'Daniel ahead.

Johnson lost, and with O'Daniel in the U.S. Senate, Stevenson was elected governor. Later Johnson told a reporter, "Jim Ferguson stole the 1941 election from me." He also told his aides, "If I ever get in another close election, I'm not going to lose it."

As good as his word, he took steps to court the people with power. He paid a call on Jim and Ma. He came with hat in hand and (to quote a Texas expression) a butter-wouldn't-melt-in-his-mouth smile. Johnson told them that he couldn't feel any hatred toward them because, in 1933, Mrs. Ferguson had given Johnson's father a job that he needed badly. Johnson further hoped that they would see their way clear to support him in the future.

Three years later Jim suffered a stroke. His health deteriorated rapidly. He lost weight from 230 pounds to 100. Some said he had deteriorated mentally to the same degree.

Ouida's biography of her mother and father told another story. As her father lay dying in his Austin home, he wanted to talk to Governor Coke Stevenson, whom he had backed for election. Ma called him to come, but Stevenson said, "I understand Jim's lost his mind."

Appalled, Ma protested, "He hasn't lost his mind as much as you think."

But Stevenson was too busy to come to see his dying friend and supporter.

According to the Fergusons' younger daughter, Dorrace, Ma was furiously angry. She vowed, "I'll cut his throat someday."

In 1948 Lyndon Johnson was running again for Senate. This time he found himself in a very close race against Coke Stevenson. He called on Ma Ferguson. She called her friend Archer Parr of Duval County, telling him how Stevenson had treated Jim in his last days.

Archer spoke to his son George, and the rest is history to be discussed in the next chapter.

History's Summation

In the wild world of Texas politics, no one can doubt that Ma Ferguson was her husband's partner. How much was her doing and how much his, no one will ever know. Some believe that she was totally without any political sense at all—"a college-educated, devoutly religious, well-bred woman who was about as political as peach cobbler." Some insist that she was just as savvy as he was. Some even believe that she was the "power behind [his] throne" throughout his terms.

Undoubtedly, she did many venal and illegal things during her two administrations. She likely found her political strength lay in pretending that she knew nothing about the political manipulations at which her husband excelled. No one can doubt that she had a purely selfish agenda that included vindicating her husband and restoring the family fortunes. In this she was only partially successful.

She could have sat down and refused to run when Jim told her that he'd entered her name in the primary. From the way he had been mauled by the press and the legislature, she would have seen that politics was not for the polite or the sheltered. Instead, she accepted the responsibility and with it the burden of the poor and the downtrodden. Whatever the truth of her stewardship, her four years in office saw the Klan destroyed,

Miriam Amanda Wallace Ferguson

"bread bonds" for the destitute issued, and the Texas economy saved by her closing the banks.

As she once said, "I am only trying to lift a burden that is hard to bear."

"The Duke of Duval"

George Berham Parr

"... contrary to rumors that have been circulated, I have always played the political game open and aboveboard."

The Way It Worked

After the Civil War, Texas suffered long in the grip of Reconstruction Governor E. J. Davis. When Texans were allowed to vote him out of office, they had to send in Rip Ford with his Cavalry of the West. Only by a combination of intimidation and main force did the despised Yankee leave the capitol.

In 1875 the legislature wrote a constitution that considerably weakened the executive branch of the state government. Its provisions left the governor with no cabinet to initiate policies and implement programs. Every office is elected independent of every other office. There is no pairing on the ballot of governor and lieutenant governor as with president and vice president of the United States.

Many times in recent years people of different parties have held the two top executive offices in the state. Governor George Bush (now president) and Lieutenant-Governor Rick Perry were from different parties. When Perry assumed the governor's chair, he switched party affiliation in an effort to promote unity and demonstrate his desire to represent all the people.

In law enforcement the state attorney general has no power to prosecute unless called upon to do so. Every county is an independent island. The richest man, the strongest man, or the largest employer can propose a candidate whose only qualification is his unquestioning loyalty to his boss. If ever a vote might possibly go against him, the appointed election judges can be made to see the desirability of recounting the votes. If some ballots are lost or gained in the process, who is available to check?

Furthermore, any disagreement, any challenge by the opposition is largely ignored. All power and discretion rests with prosecutors elected locally under the watchful eyes of the higher officials. Beyond them is no recourse. The overriding goal of those who are *in* is simply to endure.

Archie Parr, born in 1860 and orphaned as an infant, was fifteen years old when the state government was revised.

By 1891 he had drifted into Duval County where he married and bought a modest cattle ranch. He and his wife had three sons and three daughters.

As the nineteenth century turned into the twentieth, Duval was an unprepossessing place with a widely spread population engaged in farming and ranching. Like the rest of the South Texas counties, its nominal two-party system existed pretty much independent of anything that went on in Austin. A minority of citizens of English and European ancestry, most relatively new to the state, lived in and around the county seat of San Diego.

The much larger Hispanic population, estimated at ninety percent, was every one a Texan and a United States citizen. Most had much older ties to the land. Yet they were known as Mexicans. On the ranches of South Texas, they were serfs to the Anglo landowners, whom they recognized as their *patrones*.

The situation was waiting for a strong man—a boss—who could take over the county and control it with remarkably little trouble. Such a man was Archer Parr. As foreman of one of Duval County's large ranches and later owner of a small ranch of his own, he had taken the trouble to become fluent in Spanish and to demonstrate a respect for the Mexican culture. The Mexicans who worked for him appreciated his interest and his fairness.

He found a way to utilize their loyalty that others had overlooked. In 1898 he ran for and was duly elected county commissioner as a conservative Democrat.

Within the next two years, Parr developed a successful formula for staying in that position. It was his own version of boss rule—simple but effective. As Archie explained to his sons, it was as follows:

Rule 1: Control the election of every local public official.

Rule 2: Use local government to provide jobs and handouts for your friends and to punish your enemies.

Rule 3: Help yourself to as much tax money as you can get away with.

He was elected again in 1900. Everyone was pleased with him. He was *el patrón* who became, within a very few years, an important man in the county.

In 1904 the legislators passed the poll tax law to disenfranchise all but the well-to-do. In a time when $30 a month was a living wage, the poll tax was $1.75 for state and county, plus $1.00 for city. A total of $2.75 was too expensive for most to pay. Poor dirt farmers and ranchers hardly ever saw a dollar, much less nearly three. They could not afford to vote.

The Hispanic workers for the Anglo ranchers had even less money. They were paid no more than a pittance because homes of the most meager sorts were provided for them. In most cases they were unable to speak English. These men and women lived lives as separate from the Anglos as if they were south of the Rio Grande. They certainly could not pay poll taxes.

To everyone's surprise on Election Day in Duval County when their *patrón* sought re-election and control, he rounded them up. To everyone he handed a poll tax receipt. They were taken into town and given ballots, which they marked exactly as Archie told them.

The poll tax did nothing to diminish his power. In fact, it strengthened it. Availing himself of Duval County money, Archie Parr paid all his Hispanics' poll taxes. That those taxes were paid with county tax money intended for schools and public works was never mentioned. He simply cycled the money through the system. Since the Hispanics could never have voted if he hadn't done so, his action never bothered Archie's conscience. He was, from that time on, a very important man in Duval County.

His tax triumph served only to whet his appetite.

In 1907 John Cleary, the Duval County tax collector, was murdered with a double-barrel load from a shotgun. Two prominent Republicans, who were competing with Cleary over oil rights, and the deputy sheriff of the county were suspected of the deed.

In the confusion of charge and countercharge, Archie Parr was able to seize real power as interim country treasurer. He became the provider of jobs—both real and imaginary—for the unemployed. Contracts went for inflated prices with kickbacks to Parr. County road and bridge crews swelled, at least on paper. Many men never worked a day, but all were paid and Parr saw to it that all were grateful. In many cases the only qualification for a favor was a poll tax receipt.

In fact, no one failed to pay the poll tax. Every legal citizen, living or in some cases, recently dead, created a voter base that would have been the envy of other more heavily populated counties had the news gotten out.

Moreover, no one failed to vote in Duval County as Archie wished. He stationed armed deputy sheriffs at polling places to be sure that everyone voted. If the voter was illiterate, the resourceful politician provided a thoughtful service. The ballot was handed to the voter already marked, so that the man could drop it in and go on about his business.

No one objected.

As the years drifted by, paternalism, corruption, and fear controlled the elections. Voters who needed cash for groceries or doctor bills could count on Parr. If a voter needed a job, Parr could put anyone's name on the payroll and prompt the county treasurer to hand over cash or a check. The only requirement for such security was to walk into a large room in the courthouse, be handed a numbered paper ballot, sit down at a bare table, and mark the proper exes in full view of the election judge appointed by Archie Parr.

In 1914 he was elected to the state senate. Clearly, he was a man on his way up in the world.

Some would have said he'd climbed too high. When he rose to state level, a serious investigation was instituted. That his long and colorful reign had been marked by shoot-downs in the streets of San Diego, doctored elections, and the frequent unaccountable disappearance of large sums of tax money was well known. He was ordered to appear in Nueces County before a grand jury.

Unfortunately for the prosecutors, an audit of Duval County was forestalled in the early morning hours of August 11, 1914, by fire. The old wooden courthouse burned to the ground. County officials when questioned admitted sadly that it contained all the records that were to come under scrutiny. The only recourse for the prosecutors was to fume and threaten—and move on to something else.

Since Governor James Ferguson, a longtime friend of Parr's, controlled the state government, Texas indeed shrugged her shoulders and ignored what occurred in Duval County.

On another occasion when a grand jury actually met in Corpus Christi, it found plenty of election fraud but no evidence that it had affected any race for a federal office. Parr seemed immune even from investigation from Washington, D.C.

In 1918 when Parr again ran for office, Duval County, with an electorate of under 1,000 voters, mustered 1,303 votes for Parr, just 118 more than he needed to defeat his opponent. It was an amazing victory snatched as it was from the jaws of defeat.

Across Texas the morning after the election, news analysts were quick to note that—other than Parr—everyone who had supported former governor James Ferguson was defeated statewide. Although the Democratic Party leader was impeached on charges of perjury and misuse of public funds, the Duke of Duval, as he was coming to be called, survived.

For the next ten years, so consistent were Parr's wins that any Democrat facing a close election anywhere in Texas would strategically beat a path to Duval County, where he could procure a harvest of votes to put him over the top.

The Heir Apparent

George Parr was the second in a dynasty of power that ruled Duval County for almost the entire twentieth century. With his father, who retained his senate seat, and his older brother Givens, who was county judge, they possessed most of the wealth and maintained much of the power in their private domain.

Unlike Archie, who came up by his bootstraps, they were college educated and should have been enlightened men. Far and away the wealthiest and most powerful men in Duval County, they would have been able to bestow unparalleled prosperity and civility on the people living on their sprawling semidesert ranchland. Instead their rule was one of intrigue, oppression, and violence.

George's saga is one of the more amazing in Texas and American history. His power stretched beyond the tiny county seat of San Diego to neighboring counties, to the state house in Austin, to the Congress in Washington, and eventually to the White House itself.

He assumed Archie's mantle of political boss as one "to the manner born." Far from being daunted by outside intervention, he weathered it or ignored it. However, even Parr's fiefdom could not entirely stave off the twentieth century's encroachment.

In 1934 he came under investigation by the Internal Revenue Service. Somehow he had neglected to pay taxes on a $25,000 payoff from a Houston highway contractor. He was convicted and sentenced to a probated sentence of two years. Arrogant and sure of himself, he considered the whole experience a waste of taxpayer money that he could use in much better ways.

In the same year Archie needed the votes from Cameron and Hidalgo Counties in order to win his re-election to the state senate. George went to Robert Kleberg, general manager of the massive King Ranch, to put his father into the senate seat again. He needed the support of the grandson of the King. Unfortunately, Archie had chosen to champion construction of the new national Highway 77, whose route would cut through the ranch.

Kleberg, whose own kingdom was threatened, refused to approve, and subsequently Archie lost the election. George blamed the King Ranch although his own crooked dealings probably lost more votes than Kleberg's approval would have won. He vowed to get even no matter how long it took. Like a coiled rattlesnake in the shade of a massive prickly pear, he bided his time.

In 1936 George's arrogance proved his undoing. After a long list of violations that included assault, fraud, payoffs, and failure to report to his probation officer, his probation was revoked. He went to federal prison in El Reno, Oklahoma, for ten months. The experience toughened him at the same time it utterly failed to knock any arrogance out of him.

So strong was the Duval County machine that when he was released in April 1937, the young duke resumed his seat of power as if nothing had happened. Lesser men would have been discouraged by the loss of so many privileges. From that day forward he had no right to vote, nor could he hold public office. He could own neither firearms nor federally insured banks.

Unchastened, George Parr ignored the law. As for the office, he brushed its loss aside, saying, "A political officeholder is nothing but an office boy." When he stepped through the door of the precinct, the election judge bowed and scraped. Parr voted in every election because no one in Duval County would have thought of denying him a ballot.

Like a man drunk with power or a royal duke in his own forest, he hunted with his extensive gun collection, including an AR-15, the deadly assault rifle that was the standard American infantry weapon. Brazenly in broad daylight he shot deer on his own ranches as well as others in the area. Ranchers heard and saw him in his personal helicopter, a sizable arsenal within easy reach. They chose to look the other way rather than "mess with" the Duke of Duval.

Indeed in those days Texans were generally hostile toward everything that had to do with the "U.S. gov'ment." Fresh in everyone's memory was the federal government's taking control of the East Texas oil field. Governor Miriam A. "Ma" Ferguson, the former governor's wife, referred to the martial law as a "reign of terror," which had disturbed local residents "in mind and spirit." She had further accused Secretary of the Interior Harold Ickes of taking "hundreds of thousands of barrels of oil," thereby costing the state thousands of dollars daily in lost tax revenues.

Anti-U.S. government sentiment was high, and any man who fought it—even if he was guilty of shady dealings—was a hero. Indeed, a certain mystique now attached itself to George Parr. Like a romantic outlaw, people watched with something like grins on their faces as he steered his big Chrysler along the highway, flew his helicopter through the burning blue sky, or galloped his blooded horse over the Texas prairie.

No one really wanted him to be caught again. After all was said and done, he hadn't done anything to be punished by Texans. He became more popular than ever in their eyes. The federal government was his nemesis. "If George could thumb his nose at it, more power to him," they said.

Only the banks, the most conservative institutions in the country, brought him up short. He needed them to support his power. Banks were an absolute necessity to launder the millions of dollars of tax revenue he had at his disposal. Unfortunately for him, less than a decade after the crash of '29, they were powerfully regulated. Even using subterfuge, his ownership of a bank would be dangerous. Federal law enforcement had already demonstrated that it had no respect for his power.

For six more years, while Duval County's young Anglo and Hispanic men went off to fight in World War II, George struggled with legal disability and disenfranchisement. Finally in 1943, disgusted with pussyfooting around, he sought a presidential pardon to restore his rights of citizenship.

The first step was to apply to his congressman, who happened to be Richard Mifflin Kleberg, the elder brother of King Ranch general manager Robert Kleberg. Why he expected that it would be given is unknown. Perhaps he was so impressed with his own self-worth that he could not imagine anyone denying him.

While Parr seemed to have forgotten his anger at Robert's refusal to throw his support for Archie, neither Kleberg brother had forgotten Parr's refusal to vote against Highway 77 that now bisected their property. "Mr. Dick" declined to lend his name to his larcenous neighbor.

On the short end of the stick in the game of *quid pro quo*, George's fury knew no bounds. He considered now that both Klebergs were treacherous. He was determined to be avenged, especially after the embarrassment that followed.

When the request arrived on his desk, President Franklin D. Roosevelt, a liberal Democrat and his own man, denied the pardon.

When Kleberg ran for congressman again in 1944, George handpicked a war hero to challenge him. John E. Lyle Jr. had served in Europe. His war record was nothing to write home about, but he was one of "Our Boys in Uniform." With George's backing and the almost unanimous vote of Duval County, Kleberg lost by a wide margin.

When Roosevelt's victory was assured, Lyle applied again to the president for George's pardon. Accompanying the application were letters of recommendation from all of the powerful officeholders in the state who had coincidentally observed Kleberg's defeat with wary, cynical eyes. Texas Secretary of State Bob Barker even addressed Roosevelt as "Dear Franklin."

Only Governor Coke Stevenson had the courage not to endorse George. He would soon have ample cause to regret his integrity.

Whether the endorsements would have done any good is moot. Roosevelt died, and on February 20, 1946, Harry S. Truman, a political conservative, who owed much of his advancement in politics to "boss rule" by the Pendergast machine of Kansas City, granted George Parr his pardon.

Payback Time

The stroke of the presidential pen removed the federal banking regulators from Parr's neck. No longer would they have any authority to exclude him from FDIC-insured banks.

He was back in the saddle again, his power unrestrained. That power would change the entire nation.

In July 1948 Congressman Lyndon Baines Johnson was running against Coke Stevenson for the U.S. Senate. The popular governor had no idea what was about to happen to him. Not only had he incurred George's wrath, but he had angered the former governor Ma Ferguson as well. Behind the backs of the major players in the senatorial race, she made a call to the Duke.

In the primary that summer, Stevenson outpolled Johnson by more than 71,000 votes. The race would have been over despite Johnson's 4,622 votes in Duval County except that a third candidate in the race, George Peddy, received enough votes to deny Stevenson the majority.

A runoff had to be conducted in August.

Johnson, always the consummate politician, was well organized. He sent his campaign workers in ahead of him to organize barbecues, town hall meetings, any kind of assemblies he could find to listen to his message. At the height of the activities he would fly in by a helicopter he referred to as the "Johnson City Windmill." It usually landed in full sight of most of the attendees.

Out he would climb, tall, long-limbed, rawboned, the image of Texas down to the cowboy boots. Suit coat over his arm, tie loose, shirtsleeves rolled up, hat tipped back on his head, he would stride toward them, big hand outstretched and smile a mile wide. He created a character that said, "I'm one of you. I'm here to do my best for you. I don't have to put on any airs when I tell you the truth."

The race against the more dignified, reserved Stevenson, whose detractors called him "Calculatin' Coke," got close and closer. Johnson played his last card. As so many had done before him, he flew to Duval County to beg an audience with the Duke.

Though Parr was willing to support Johnson for more than one reason, unfortunately, he had voted just about every eligible voter, living and dead, he could muster in Duval County. He had literally no more names to pull from his hat.

But he would do his best for Lyndon. He wanted him in the Senate for Texas. He wanted his revenge on Stevenson, who had refused to endorse him when he had applied for the presidential pardon from Roosevelt. And his daddy wanted him to do what Ma Ferguson asked him to do.

Jim Wells County shares the boundary line with Duval. Only ten miles from San Diego is Alice, the county seat. One hour after the closing of the polls, the election judge of Precinct 13 went to the town newspaper office. The final count of Box 13 was listed in the paper the next day as 765 votes for Lyndon Johnson and 60 for Coke Stevenson.

Six days later, when the vote was reported to the county Democratic Executive Committee, to everyone's considerable amazement Lyndon Johnson had acquired 200 more votes. His figures had increased to 965 from 765. The margin was just enough for Stevenson to lose the Democratic primary. Since the election in November was a foregone conclusion to go Democratic, Lyndon Baines Johnson would be the next senator from Texas.

Of course, Coke Stevenson's constituents wanted a look at that ballot box. They were refused copies of the record. Stevenson himself was allowed to look at the list of voters but not to take notes. One thing that he noted was that the names of the first 841 voters, including all those who had voted for him, were written in black ink. The last 200 were written in blue ink. Furthermore, the "9" in 965 was an overwrite. A black seven clearly showed under a blue nine.

The newly elected county chairman Harry Lee Adams did get to copy some names at random from the list of 200. The first thing he noted was that beginning with Mrs. Enriqueto Acero through Louis Salinas, every name was in strict alphabetical order.

Later, when Mrs. Acero was asked under oath in a Fort Worth courtroom whether or not she had voted, she replied unequivocally that she had not. She also testified that to her knowledge she was the only person named Enriqueto Acero in Jim Wells County.

Later when Eugenio Solis, the last voter whose name was written in black, was questioned, he reported that he had voted just before the polls closed at seven P.M. He reported that when he left, no one else was there.

Still when all the votes in the state were counted, including the 200 from Box 13, Lyndon Johnson had won by 87 votes out of a million cast, thereby earning himself the nickname "Landslide Lyndon."

One can only imagine the excitement that must have ensued at the polling site of Precinct 13 when within seconds before the polls closed 200 people suddenly arrived. What a screeching of tires and a slamming of car doors! Horns must have blared as perhaps 100 to 150 vehicles tried to park on the ordinarily quiet street. People must have rushed to the doors and shoved each other aside as they fought to be first in line to vote for their senatorial choice.

Once inside, they must have realized what an imposition such confusion would have placed on the election judge, who had only an hour to get the box down to the newspaper. With admirable presence of mind 200 perfect strangers arranged themselves in alphabetical order to facilitate their balloting. With only forty-five or fifty minutes to spare, they voted. Four and five people a minute cast ballots unerringly as fast as they could sit down at the tables and mark them. Then like a flock of sparrows they fled, leaving the election judge nothing to do but close the box and carry it down to the newspaper. Surely, their appearance and departure must have so amazed the man that he failed until later to include their names and change his own vote total.

On September 15 Coke Stevenson presented the suspect information his constituents had laboriously gathered to the United States District Court of the Northern District of Texas. Judge T. Whitfield Davidson granted a restraining order preventing the Texas secretary of state from certifying Lyndon Johnson as the winner. An investigation began with many of the most prominent lawyers in Texas participating.

It was doomed from the beginning. Key witnesses had suddenly gone missing. Neither the former election judge nor the committee secretary could be found. Likewise, all three poll lists required by law had also disappeared by the time the case went to court.

Eventually the contest went to the U.S. Supreme Court where, at Congressman Lyndon Baines Johnson's request, Justice Hugo Black issued an order preventing further investigation of the vote fraud.

Lyndon Johnson had won the Senate seat he coveted. He never apologized for nor commented on his victory. Certainly the word "fraud" never passed his lips. Instead, he faced the public with brazen arrogance.

He took a lesson from the man who had given him a seat shared by only ninety-six lawmakers in the world. Power and influence were his. He sought to exercise them like the man who had given them to him—George Parr.

The Glare of the Spotlight

On September 27, 1948, *Time* magazine marveled how "Parr could deliver...Duval County's return: Johnson 4,622; Stevenson 40." The editors of the magazine had not looked far enough. They would have thought it much more marvelous had they seen that in Stevenson's gubernatorial run, Parr had delivered for him. When Stevenson had refused to write a letter to Roosevelt, he had sealed his own fate.

As Richard and Robert Kleberg had found out before him, Stevenson learned that George Parr never forgave or forgot. At a nod from him, his entire electorate—the power base so carefully nurtured by his father—had done his will. It had reversed itself.

While the nation never received that piece of information, the notoriety of the election was the beginning of the end for Parr. Instead of retiring quietly until the hubbub died, he sought the spotlight. Perhaps he began to entertain state and national political ambitions of his own.

When within a year the Duval County judge died, Parr had himself appointed to his unfilled term. He might have begun a steady march up the ladder to the United States Congress. He might have reached even farther than that, but his personal life interfered.

His wife divorced him in a very public way. She had divorced and remarried George in 1933 and 1934. This time Thelma Duckworth Parr, long-suffering and long neglected, meant to make it stick.

And stick it to him she did. She received $1,000 a month child support for their daughter as well as $425,000 in cash and her community property rights to real estate and oil and gas interests. Up to that time Parr had maintained the facade of a rancher of modest means.

Speculation rose as to where all that money had come from. *Collier's* magazine did an exposé detailing Parr's interest in 200 producing oil wells, controlling interests in the San Diego State Bank in Duval County and the Texas State Bank of Alice in Jim Wells County, and controlling interest in the San Diego Distributing Company, the only beer wholesaler in the county. No one could get a license to sell beer except from the county judge, who was also George Parr.

Collier's also noted that he owned the Duval Construction Company, which had been awarded every road-building, repair, and improvement project in Duval County for fifteen years.

They noted his ranch comprised 70,000 acres where his "palatial San Diego mansion is situated on walled, lushly landscaped grounds with swimming pool, multiple garage and large servants' quarters. Nearby are stables for his 25 blooded quarter horses—and his private race track, complete with automatic starting chutes and judges' stand."

More revealing to the nation were the contrasting descriptions and pictures of "Latin shantytowns" scattered around Duval County. The magazine called them "dilapidated one- and two-room shacks crazily crowded together, frequently without plumbing or electricity."

Even as the national magazine reported the vicious, unprincipled discrepancies between the Duke and his people, a "Freedom Party" reform movement was taking shape within the county. World War II had taken a sizable number of Duval County's sons into military service. They had left as ignorant, barely literate farm boys. In 1945 they returned as well-trained, disciplined free men, many with heroes medals gleaming on their chests. They were no longer afraid of guns or bullies.

They wanted their say in government.

There was still a poll tax to be paid, but $2.75 didn't loom so large after forty years of inflation. Moreover, they were willing to take personal risks for it as their grandfathers and fathers had never done.

They could not gain the power without a struggle. Parr retaliated with all the considerable weapons at his command. Small business owners allied against the "Old Party" were ruined financially. Their parking lots were blocked; their customers were harassed by Duval County deputy sheriffs. Their children were shunned by their classmates. Welfare recipients were warned that their names would be taken off the roles if they traded with the wrong merchants.

To Parr's amazement the new Freedom Party did not surrender. He intensified his attack.

Casualties in the last half of the decade were heavy. Sam Smithwick, the deputy sheriff of Jim Wells County, murdered W. H. "Bill" Mason, the outspoken program director of Alice's radio station. The deputy went to jail, but Sheriff H. T. Sain, a Parr man, lost the next election.

People thought that such a defeat would send a message to Parr to back off, but instead he retaliated with more viciousness. Harassment of citizens increased. Every official in Duval County was in Parr's pocket.

In Austin, Governor Allan Shivers, his attorney general Price Daniel, and his secretary of state John Ben Shepperd were being forced to look at the corruption and near anarchy that existed barely two hundred miles to the south.

In the 1950 election, Parr was determined to be rid of Judge Sam Reams of the 79th Judicial District. The judge was under the impression that he was running unopposed. Parr quietly ordered a write-in campaign against his nemesis and withheld the ballots until the votes from the other three counties were counted.

Their results showed Reams had captured more than 4,000 votes. But where were the returns from Duval? Six days later the official county vote came in. Parr's write-in candidate had received 4,730 votes, 200 more than Reams's total.

It was a flagrant attempt to steal the election by a thief so arrogant that he seemed to have lost all sense of decorum. Though they might have a tiger by the tail, Shivers, Daniel, and Shepperd had no choice but to refuse to certify the surprise candidate. When Parr seemed about to retaliate, they dared him to force the issue in Austin.

Realizing he would have to fight off his home turf, Parr backed down, but the judge, the governor, the attorney general, the secretary of state, and the Duke of Duval were engaged in a battle that would last for an entire decade.

Immediately after his election, Reams convened a grand jury to investigate fraud in Duval County. Its deliberations were an unfortunate example that the wheels of the gods grind slowly.

While the rest of the United States looked on in awe, Texans loved it. Politics had never been so exciting.

The Gloves Come Off

Indeed, the dukedom seemed invincible until September 8, 1952, when a crack appeared. The Old Party suffered a defection. At about nine o'clock in the evening, Jake Floyd, an activist lawyer for the Freedom Party in Jim Wells County, received a warning phone call from Nago Alaniz, Parr's lawyer. Alaniz had been allied with Parr for years, but what was about to happen went too far for him. A pair of professional killers had been imported from Mexico to kill Floyd and Judge Sam Reams. According to Alaniz, Mario Sapet, a special deputy in Duval County, led them.

Floyd hung up the phone and immediately sought the sheriff's support. He took a taxi to the Jim Wells County jail. His quick action saved his own life, but he returned home that night to find his son Buddy, who looked just like him, dying of a gunshot wound in the driveway. The murder weapon was recovered and found to be Sapet's property. While the triggermen escaped to Mexico, Sapet was tried, found guilty, and sentenced to ninety-nine years. Alaniz was tried as an accomplice but was acquitted by the jury because of his call to Floyd.

George Parr was rumored to have paid for Sapet's defense, but no connection was ever discovered. When interviewed by the *Corpus Christi Caller,* the Duke insisted, "My conscience is absolutely clear..."

The battle intensified throughout the 1950s. In the 1952 election Freedom Party candidates filed for every office in Duval County. Parr's harassment and intimidation grew more intense. Probably as a result of fear among the voting populace, Reams lost the next election.

A U.S. Border Patrol agent was found shot to death in a burning automobile on a Duval County road. His murder is still unsolved, but it gave Shivers the opening he needed to send in the Texas Rangers. They were a presence at every political rally thereafter, a bar against intimidation and harassment. Their captain, Alfred Y. Allee, started a vigorous investigation into Buddy Floyd's death as well as the death of the Border Patrol agent.

Meanwhile, Price Daniel sent in an investigative team to search for evidence of corruption in the official records of Duval County and its school districts, the tax collection records, and the disbursal of such public funds. Along the way the Internal Revenue Service and the Post Office Department joined the state officers. The weather wasn't the only thing in Duval County that was hot, hot, hot.

The Duke struck back with his considerable resources. Crucial records disappeared. No one in any office co-operated in any way. Still, the strain was telling on Parr. In February 1954, brimming with fury and frustration, he carried a pistol to a political rally in Alice and provoked an argument with a member of the Freedom Party. The confrontation made the *New York Times.* "Pistols, Rangers, Indictments Mix In Old-Time Texas Political Row."

 The next month Parr's hand-picked and hand-elected judge, C. Woodrow Laughlin, who had replaced Reams, was removed from office. Though Laughlin was replaced by an appointment from North Texas where Parr had no influence, Parr didn't hesitate to retaliate. He filed a civil rights suit against Texas Ranger Captain Alfred Allee in federal court. His testimony was that the ranger had tried to kill him.

 Though Parr finally withdrew the suit, Allee felt no gratitude. "[George Parr's] a dangerous man who would do anything under the sun, and I don't treat a tiger like I do a rabbit."

 For the next six years, grand juries and state and federal officials whittled away at Parr's dukedom. Parr faced them boldly with the almighty in-your-face arrogance that won him open admiration at the same time it disgusted and frightened people. Governors and attorneys general came and went. Rangers and border patrolmen were transferred or resigned.

 But Parr went on forever.

 He had his nephew and adopted son Archer Parr elected sheriff. Later he missed getting the new "Archie" elected to the state senate by only a few votes. The national magazines and newspapers carried sensational stories of "keeping people on the public payroll at substantial salaries for doing nothing, handing out contracts to the group for goods and services rendered to the county, cashing checks made out to fictitious persons or to persons who did not earn the money and never saw the checks."

 More investigations and orders followed. George was forced to divest himself of his two banks. Of course, the sales were to his friends.

He was indicted for income tax evasion, but the amounts owed ($85,000 for three years) were small. He could pay those with a shrug and a sneer. But where were the hundreds of thousands of Duval County tax dollars that had disappeared?

Gradually a few rats began to desert the ship, which if not sinking was certainly taking on water. Young Archie resigned as sheriff and entered law school at the University of Texas. The Benavides School District's bookkeeper was granted immunity from prosecution and ordered to testify before the state grand jury. Most unsettling to George was the desertion of Dan Tobin Jr., a friend whose father had stood with George's father.

In 1956 George won the office of sheriff, but the election committee declared him ineligible because of the money he owed the county. He swore he was deeply in debt to the tune of nearly two million dollars. At the end of that year, he was convicted on charges of mail fraud since the tax notices for the Benavides Independent Schools had been mailed out, but the district had not received the moneys. For two years the appeal battles raged—all the way to the Supreme Court of the United States.

Strange Bedfellows Indeed

Then it all went away.

In 1960 the Supreme Court reversed the decisions of the lower courts stating there was "no evidence... that the taxes assessed were excessive..." and their use of the mail was not "for the purpose of executing the scheme." The reason for this sudden shift in the wind was obvious in the light of national politics.

In 1960 John F. Kennedy was elected president of the United States. His vice president was Parr's old friend and debtor "Landslide" Lyndon Johnson. Duval County voted the straight Democratic ticket. Moreover, John Connally in his first run for governor saw nearly one hundred percent of Duval County go for him.

The Duke of Duval suddenly had friends in exceedingly high places.

The investigations collapsed or were withdrawn. In March 1963 U.S. Attorney General Robert F. Kennedy ordered the dismissal of the government's 1954 tax evasion case after a "thorough" review of the indictment.

George was free of the threat of criminal prosecution. In a way that must have seemed downright miraculous, he could return to "business as usual."

But the greatest miracle of all for him occurred only eight months later. Kennedy was assassinated in Dallas, and George Parr's friend, the direct recipient of his most notorious political manipulations, ascended to the highest office in the land.

In the 1964 election Archer Parr, a newly elected Duval County judge, was a Texas delegate to the Democratic Convention. Moreover, a new judicial district was created out of Duval, Starr, and Zapata Counties. George became a trusted confidant and sometime confederate of the powerful Carrillo family, who had control of the local judiciary.

The Old Party reclaimed every aspect of Duval County government, and George and Archer created a new governmental entity—the Duval County Conservation and Reclamation District. For a decade they would run the county for fun and profit.

George Parr had a right to expect that the Democrats would stay in power for at least sixteen years. John F. Kennedy was the youngest man ever elected to the presidency at that time. Lyndon Johnson was hale and hearty. Robert Kennedy was only in his thirties. The country was in love with them all.

The assassination in Dallas changed everything.

George Berham Parr

The Wheels of the Gods

The assassination that had seemed so propitious for Duval County signaled the beginning of the end. Johnson was now president, but his heart was bad. Broken and dying, he did not run for re-election. In his bid for the presidency, Robert Kennedy was assassinated, and Johnson's vice president, Hubert Humphrey, was defeated.

The man in the White House was Richard Nixon, a bitter Republican who considered that Kennedy had stolen the election from him in 1960.

On May 22, 1972, with a promise of immunity, one Carl Stautz signed a twenty-three-page affidavit that marked the beginning of the end for George Parr's reign in Duval County. Witnessed by two special agents of the Internal Revenue Service, it detailed construction done by the Triangle Construction Company for the San Diego and Benavides Independent School Districts. The checks totaling $2,500,000 were payable to cash.

Those sums were brought to the attention of the CID, the Criminal Investigation Division of the IRS. Every audited taxpayer should know how to react to an introduction of a CID agent into his case. Phone immediately for the best criminal lawyer you can afford. You know the prison doors are yawning for you.

Stautz reported that he had used most of the money to pay kickbacks to the county school officials. The principle payment had been to George Parr.

It was the end. Too little time had passed since the investigations had been called off. Too many people still with the service remembered the Duke. Too many still smarted from the frustrations and failures attached to his name. They wanted his head.

Stautz for his part was scared to death. Not so many years before, people had been shot down in driveways and burned to death in cars. With the record of past county crimes to look at, the CID took him seriously when he demanded protection.

George Parr had been the sole power in Duval County for nearly fifty years, having assumed the mantle of his father in 1926. He was at times smart and feisty as ever, but at times he seemed delusional. Once he called a deputy to confess that he had killed his current wife Eva and that her blood was all over the floor. When the deputy arrived, nothing was to be found.

When he was brought to trial in March 1974, no one expected that he would be found guilty. The entire case was built on technicalities and one crook's testimony. Greater charges than these had been dismissed before. But the Republicans were in the White House and in the state house in Austin. The power was stretched thin as barbed wire.

People who would never have uttered a sound a few years before stepped forward to testify. In the end Parr was found guilty and sentenced to the federal penitentiary.

A year later he was still free on $75,000 bond. On March 24, 1975, the New Orleans circuit court affirmed his conviction. He was scheduled to appear in federal court in Corpus Christi on the afternoon of March 31, 1975.

Ride the Man Down

When he failed to appear, his bond was revoked. Local, state, and federal authorities combined to stage a Wild West manhunt. Speculation was that he would flee to Mexico. He was wealthy, he spoke Spanish fluently, he lived less than a hundred miles from the border. Furthermore, he had been to prison before. He had stated many times that he would never go back.

The lawmen were further alarmed by the knowledge that he had in his possession a .45 semiautomatic pistol and an AR-15 designed specifically to kill men in combat. Its

George Berham Parr

high-velocity 5.66mm ammunition was contained in twenty- and thirty-round clips that could stop a police car or bring down a helicopter.

On the morning of April 1, just such a helicopter flew over his ranch where a cluster of lawmen in various uniforms waited at the gate. Also on hand were reporters from the *Corpus Christi Caller* and the Associated Press. No one moved. No one had the stomach for a blazing gun battle from the bad old days of the Texas frontier. No one wanted to be first to face the Duke.

After a brief conference the helicopter lifted off again to survey the ranch. In ten minutes the men aboard sighted Parr's big Chrysler on a mound in the Julian pasture, his favorite spot on his ranch. Flanked by a windmill with a concrete water tank and a periphery of mesquite trees, it commanded a view of much of the surrounding countryside.

Warily the chopper circled, afraid of the firepower Parr was known to have. If he were going to fight, he had chosen his spot well. Finally, it swept in close enough to see through the windshield. Something brown lay on the front seat. Parr was known to have worn a brown shirt.

Still wary, they landed the helicopter seventy-five yards away. FBI Special Agent Martinez trotted up behind the car. There was no movement. He came to the passenger side and looked in. Parr was slumped on his right side. The bullet had entered his right temple and exited his left. The .45 was on his lap. The AR-15 lay on the front seat under his hand. Both weapons were found to be fully loaded. In addition there were eight clips of ammunition.

He had driven to the Julian pasture with two choices—both of which he was determined would end with his death. What thoughts went through his head, no one will ever know.

One can imagine the Duke reviewing the triumphs of his long life. He was only a couple of years shy of eighty. He undoubtedly weighed his chances of going out in a blazing gun battle shot to death by his enemies like the legendary outlaws at the end of the century in which he was born.

It was a glorious picture and probably very appealing. But suppose somehow they captured rather than killed him. He would not risk spending his last days in a prison cell. No! Better to take one last look at his kingdom, then pull the trigger.

In the end, George Parr chose not to fight that last fight.

History's Assessment

Although Archer Parr held several offices in Duval County after his adoptive father's death, he was never called the Duke. Despite convictions in the last quarter of the century for perjury and theft of county equipment, many liked and respected him as much as others despised him. He died in the hospital in Alice on November 4, 2000.

The Duke of Duval left behind a legend that still resonates in Texas. The electorate he raised and trained still votes in Texas elections. The "Old Party" is gone forever, but the "Freedom Party" flourished in adversity. Learning how to control from an exemplary machine, it became stronger and tougher.

More important beyond the strict boundaries of Duval County, the "hardest-working" senator in Congress, "Landslide" Lyndon, became the youngest majority leader in the history of that August body. In the White House, President Johnson drove through some of the most significant legislation in the history of America. His Civil Rights Act outlawed segregation, and his Equal Opportunity Act declared "war on poverty."

Ironically, it all began with Box 13.

"The Consummate Politician"

Lyndon Baines Johnson

"No President in history has been able to do all the things that he hoped he could accomplish. But that doesn't mean the job is impossible and that doesn't mean it's doomed. It is doable."

The Dealing for the Presidency

Before 1960 the politics of the United States had been confined almost exclusively to Washington, D.C. That year, through the new rapidly developing world of portable television cameras, it became the politics of the people. At the same time, Texas politics became the politics of the United States when John Fitzgerald Kennedy at forty-one and Lyndon Baines Johnson at fifty-two struck a devil's bargain that became the Democratic ticket.

That Senate Majority Leader Johnson of Texas, with almost thirty years in Washington, should have teamed with Senator Kennedy from Boston was an odd coupling. On the other hand, their combined strength created a surprisingly good political mix.

Johnson had arrived in Washington on December 7, 1931, as congressional secretary to Richard Mifflin Kleberg, a grandson of Richard King and a general manager of the enormous King Ranch. For three years Johnson served the congressman well; at the same time he learned about the political process. Those years took the place of law school. In a sense they were more absorbing, more intense, and more practical in terms of knowledge than the very best law school he could have found.

He returned to Texas in 1934 to join Maury Maverick's political run for Congress. In 1937 at the age of twenty-nine, he himself won a vacated congressional seat. He was consistently reelected to it for nine years, even as he lost a special election to the Senate despite the support of President Franklin Delano Roosevelt, who had come to know the Texan and to recognize his political acumen.

Johnson won the election the next year and rose rapidly from chairman of the Armed Services Preparedness Investigating Subcommittee to Democratic Whip to Floor Leader to Majority Leader. Even though he suffered a serious heart attack in 1955, he was a known liberal and very popular with the Democrats. He was imposingly tall and lanky with a long nose and piercing eyes. He looked like the stereotypical Texan. In the minds of many voters he was "a man to ride the river with."

However, the scion of an Irish political party from Boston had sewn up a slender majority of convention votes. Kennedy had campaigned long and hard through every state primary. He had strong ties to labor through his grandfather "Honey Fitz" Fitzgerald. He had a glamorous reputation as a PT boat commander and daredevil hero in World War II. He had received a Pulitzer Prize for *Profiles in Courage,* a book he was supposed to have written while recuperating from war wounds.

More important "as the world turned," Kennedy had matinee idol good looks. Although the seasoned politicians of the time took no notice of his blue eyes, his chiseled jaw, his wavy blonde hair, the voting public liked him instantly when the all-seeing eye of television was turned on him.

Lyndon Baines Johnson

Leapfrogging over the "way things were done" at that time, Kennedy had gone out to win most of the Democratic primaries across the country. He had superseded the patronage of smoke-filled rooms and garnered enough votes to win the nomination but nowhere near enough electoral votes to win the presidency.

The convention was in turmoil. The delegates were desperate to win back the White House after eight years of Eisenhower's extreme conservatism.

The only chance Kennedy saw was if Johnson would accept the other half of the ticket. He needed Johnson's political expertise as well as the large number of electoral votes he commanded. When Kennedy's men first approached Johnson's men with an offer of the vice-presidency, they were turned away.

As the Democratic National Convention began, the politicking was rampant on the floor. If a few swing states could be persuaded to change their votes so that Kennedy lost on the first ballot, then a floor fight would ensue. Most delegates were committed to vote as their states had instructed them but for the *first ballot only*. After that they were free to vote as they saw fit.

This convention was different from any seen before. For the first time, TV cameras operated inside the building, trained not on the reading of the platform, the dull business of certifying of the delegations, the drone of the nominating speeches, or the indiscriminate multitude waving placards and cheering. Instead, their roving eyes watched as Jack Kennedy and his brother Robert worked the floor. The commentators reminded people *sotto voce* that Kennedy's brother-in-law was the movie star Peter Lawford.

Through their eyes, the American people watched spellbound as wheeler-dealers from the Texas delegation, led by the lanky, energetic Johnson, buttonholed other state delegations. Six-feet-four, his technique was to get up close until his body actually touched and loomed over the man he was talking to. No one could stand up to him. Behind him, bald head shining, was Sam Rayburn, the formidable Speaker of the House of Representatives.

"Vote for me!" said Kennedy.

"Vote for me!" drawled Johnson.

But neither man could command enough for a majority.

One can imagine the smoke-filled rooms where the inner circles gathered to finally settle on these two men and plan campaigns for them.

"Deliver Texas." Johnson could do that.

"Turn out the unions." Kennedy could do that.

Sam Rayburn, practically a god in Texas politics, is rumored to have convinced Johnson to accept the second place on the ticket, but not before Kennedy himself had visited Rayburn and gotten his support. Rayburn is supposed to have suggested to his protégé Johnson that the Democratic Party could not win because of Eisenhower's aura transferring to Nixon. Kennedy would be defeated. The popular wisdom of the day was that the stigma of loser would finish him for presidential politics.

Johnson, who would be running for senator in the same election, would still be senator, still be majority leader, and still be a clear favorite to run in 1964, when the country would surely vote the conservative Nixon out of office.

So the ticket was struck. Each man actively disliked the other. Johnson had been raised on a farm and educated in a country school. Kennedy had had everything handed to him. Rather than cooperate, they looked as if they might rather face each other in the main aisle with six-shooters.

Elder Democrats privately wondered what they had wrought. They were leery of their "young guns."

Once nomination was decided and the campaigning began in earnest, presidential debates were proposed. Again the all-seeing eye of television influenced the people. For the first time candidates appeared in close-ups, "warts and all." When Kennedy met Nixon in the first nationally televised debates ever held, more than just issues were decided.

Kennedy's American/Celtic good looks were revealed as well as his endearing Boston twang. The Democratic candidate looked like a movie star (because he had been made up like one). The same camera showed Dick Nixon's puffy jowls blackened by "five o'clock shadow." His voice was gruff and unfriendly. The Republican looked like a thug.

In November when the votes were counted, the country had voted virtually a dead heat. Not in the twentieth century had such a thing happened. Suddenly, the Electoral College and the majority party in the Senate loomed large. Some election returns were suspect. Would there be a national recount? In the end, at Eisenhower's advice, Nixon conceded rather than throw the country into voting turmoil.

And Lyndon Baines Johnson, who had been reasonably assured that Kennedy would lose, found himself in the unenviable position of vice president to a man who disliked him and for whom he had barely concealed contempt.

When Kennedy's liberal plans stalled in Congress, the chances of Johnson's recovering his career seemed far in the future and altogether negligible. The president's credibility was further tattered by a hail of gunfire and stained by a swirl of blood in the Bay of Pigs on the Cuban coast.

All might have been over for Johnson in 1964, except for a tragic day in Dallas.

Texas in His Bones

The future president was born in the Hill Country of Central Texas in the fairly broad valley of the Pedernales River. His mother, Rebekah Baines, was from Fredericksburg, a primarily German community, where she worked as an elocution teacher and newspaper reporter until she married his father, Samuel Johnson, who took her back to a farm beside his own father's on the banks of the river. Sam had been a state representative before quitting the job, which then paid $2.00 a day, to farm full time.

Lyndon Baines, their first son, was born in a frame house a hundred yards from the river. When he was four years old, his mother put him in the rural school because he was always escaping to go play with the children on the playground.

He grew up as he began—eager, intelligent. While he was never a scholar, he was a good boy. He always wanted to be the center of attention, immersed in the cultural, moral, and religious teachings of his parents and the people of that part of Texas. He was baptized by a Christian minister on the banks of the Pedernales in the summer of 1923. Johnson would refer to the experience in numerous speeches, noting humorously that the river was almost dry that year. Most Texans could relate to that, since some part of Texas needs rain almost every year.

Standing over six-feet tall and thin as a beanpole, he graduated from high school at fifteen. Although he attended Southwest Texas State Teachers College at San Marcos, south of Austin, his education was spotty. Whether he graduated is anybody's guess, but he did attend long enough to get his teaching credentials. Only two years were required to become a schoolteacher in the 1920s.

As a matter of fact, education bored him, but despite his lack of scholarly interest, he never rebelled against the authority of the teachers. That too was part of his Texas rearing. All

The Johnson homestead and birthplace as it appears today now part of the Lyndon B. Johnson National Historical Park.

his life he deferred to people who were older, better educated, and more authoritative than he. His frustrated detractors frequently accused him of hypocrisy, of "sucking up." His attitude was sincere. He was never rude or brusque with the older members of Congress whom he generally considered to be founts of knowledge and experience.

The truth was that Lyndon Baines Johnson loved older people and wanted to help them, especially when he saw them worn out, ill, impoverished, and alone as so many were as the nation became more urbanized. He also knew firsthand the power of influence in politics.

In 1930 Richard Kleberg, one of the owners and managers of his grandfather's King Ranch, ran for election to U.S. Congress. The ranch's name and reputation being sterling, he easily claimed the Democratic nomination. An affable sort, he ran his campaign with only a vague mention of issues, entertained his audiences, bought the expected Mexican votes in San Antonio and counties south, and won the statewide election in November.

He would need a congressional secretary.

What followed was a series of circumstances that exemplifies the way Texas politics works. Lyndon's father, Sam, worked for the Democratic Party in Blanco County where Welly Hopkins, an Austin lawyer, was running for state senator. Sam helped Welly win. As a favor to Sam, Welly wrote a letter to Roy Miller, the former mayor of Corpus Christi and current lobbyist for Texas Gulf Sulphur Corporation. During those years the town and the corporation were almost interlocked with the King Ranch. Roy wrote a letter to Dick Kleberg recommending Lyndon for the post.

To put the sequence simply: Sam did a job for Welly. In gratitude Welly wrote Roy. Roy wrote Dick. Dick hired Lyndon.

Texas politics as everyone understood it.

The former San Marcos schoolteacher never forgot how his first important job came about. Texas was in Johnson's bones, and from that moment on, politics was his own personal art. He was single-minded about it. He sacrificed everything to it as it consumed him.

More than perhaps any other man who has served as president, he dedicated his every waking moment to his monumental task. And he slept very little. More often than not, twenty hours a day were devoted to the complexities of the office he held and the office he sought.

Working for Dick Kleberg was the best thing that ever happened to Johnson. During his terms in the Congress, Kleberg never introduced a bill, nor spoke for or against any particular issue. He saw his job as showing up to vote on legislation introduced by the Democratic Party and attending the meetings of his one congressional committee. Otherwise, he attended social functions and played golf.

Johnson handled all Kleberg's paperwork and dealt with his constituents. He dealt with most telephone calls and answered all the mail. He often signed Kleberg's name. He did all the lobbying and soliciting in federal agencies. He cultivated political support and so began to offer policy suggestions that Kleberg almost invariably acted upon.

And Johnson met and knew everybody in town.

In effect, he became the Congressman for the Fourteenth District. And a very good congressman he was.

While serving as secretary, Johnson observed that a wife of estimable qualities was on the arm of every successful politician. In 1934 Johnson set out to meet and marry Claudia Alta Taylor whom everyone from her "Negro mammy" to the richest friends of her rich father called Lady Bird.

He had heard about her through an office secretary in Austin, and he knew her credentials. At twenty-six he had decided that he wanted to marry. Since he did not love anyone nor have time to date and court, he had decided to make a match to include all the things he did not have—old family, wealth, good breeding, gentility. Claudia Taylor had all of those "in buckets." He asked her to breakfast at the Driskill Hotel.

She has always maintained that she had not planned to keep the date, but when she walked by the hotel the next morning, she saw him waving. Of course one might ask why she walked by that particular hotel when she knew he would be sitting in the restaurant watching for her through the plate glass window. Be that as it may, he hurried out to take her arm, brought her inside, and seated her.

Almost immediately the conversation became "intense and personal." After breakfast he took her for a drive where he shared his dreams and ambitions. She had never met anyone like him. Undoubtedly, only a special few men were like him anywhere in the world. He described his life as he envisioned it living in Washington, D.C., but if he mentioned the presidency, she didn't remember. Probably that was too high for even his vaulting ambition.

By the end of the day, he had proposed marriage.

Next day he took her to San Marcos to meet his parents and then drove her down to Kingsville to the ranch to meet Alice Gertrudis King Kleberg, the congressman's mother, a *grande dame* of Texas whom Johnson had always treated with utmost deference.

By the end of the week, on his way back to Washington, D.C., he drove through Karnack, Texas, on Caddo Lake, just ten miles from the Louisiana border. There he met her father, who succumbed to the Johnson charm within minutes. On November 17 he married her, bypassing several state regulations and all but forcing an Episcopalian minister to marry them.

She gave him class; he gave her hard-driving ambition. It was a match made in a heaven called Texas. Even their initials matched—a fact that LBJ would capitalize on over and over, even going so far as to name their daughters Lynda Bird and Luci Baines.

Lady Bird always remained at his side, a vital member of the Johnson political team. He undoubtedly congratulated himself many times, especially when he discovered he had married so very much more than he thought.

He found out she was tempered steel beneath the shy, polite surface. He also discovered that, like him, she was eager to improve herself and unafraid to tackle anything. She lacked social confidence, so she began to study to gain it. All her life Lady Bird Johnson has been continually reading, learning, and growing.

For her part she must have found out early that marriage to such a volatile and basically insecure man was no bed of roses. She stayed with her husband despite his crudeness, his temper tantrums, his infidelity, and his ego trips. In the end she gained his gratitude, his respect, and finally his dependence.

With her beside him he quickly became the perfect candidate.

Lyndon Baines Johnson

The Ins and Outs

On February 23, 1937, the Congressman from the Tenth Congressional District died. The district included both Austin and Johnson City. Johnson saw his chance even though it was a long shot. The widow of a deceased congressman was traditionally offered the opportunity to declare for her husband's seat. However, Johnson's father advised him to announce his candidacy immediately.

Whether she was grief-stricken or intimidated at the thought of running against such an experienced and eager young man is unknown. The widow declined to accept the nomination. The race was thrown open. Eight candidates filed.

Johnson's platform was simple—complete support of Roosevelt's New Deal policies and programs. The 32nd president was extremely popular in that part of Texas due to the Agricultural Adjustment Act, Rural Electrification, and the Social Security Act that had convinced the poor farmers he was for them.

Lyndon worked ceaselessly to secure the party nomination and then the election. In March he opened his campaign with a radio address. While it was a failure, it taught him many things. He gave a speech too intellectual and too filled with Washington knowledge for the general public to comprehend. A week later he "changed horses" and delivered one of Roosevelt's patented "fireside chats."

Because he was only twenty-seven years old, he worked twice as hard as the other candidates. Eighteen hours a day for nearly nine months he traveled around Texas. Lady Bird contributed $10,000 of her money—a princely sum in those days—to kick off his campaign. In the end his presence won the day—his deep intense voice and Texas accent, his personalized delivery, his physical contact, and above all his superb argumentative skills. More and more of the people of his district came to recognize what a representative they would have in him.

At the climax of the campaign, while making a speech in Austin, he collapsed. Wracked by stomach pains, underweight, physically exhausted, and groggy from lack of sleep, he had pushed himself until his iron will could no longer sustain him. His friends rushed him to a hospital where the doctors removed a "hot" appendix. Hundreds probably made the special effort to vote in sympathy.

He rose from his bed with no qualms and resumed the campaign trail as if nothing had happened. While the "hot" appendix turned out to be something of a good thing, his attitude toward it was not. Forcing himself to recover as if nothing had happened began a pattern of behavior that laid the foundation for his early death.

Because he was willing to make such sacrifices, his opponents never stood a chance. He won handily and was off to Washington, this time as his own man with his socially acceptable and clever wife on his arm.

In the House of Representatives, he was frustrated within months. He was a junior congressman, the third youngest man in the House, with no power whatsoever. Moreover, power was not likely to come his way anytime soon.

Texans by virtue of their consistently Democratic Party vote returned their congressmen term after term with little or no opposition. Besides Sam Rayburn, the Speaker of the House, the chairman of the Reconstruction Finance Committee was Jesse Jones, the Houston magnate. He would go on to be Secretary of Commerce. Texans held the committee chairs of Agriculture, Interstate Commerce, Judiciary, Public Buildings and Grounds, Rivers and Harbors, and, most important, Appropriations. As a group they secured for their state money and appropriations so vast as to top the national average by twenty-seven percent.

Lyndon Baines Johnson with Lady Bird at his side "kicks off" his first Senate campaign, which he would lose because of Ferguson influence.
LBJ Library Photo Archives

Johnson could not hope to become more than he was in the House. There he was a small fish in a big pond. He felt himself destined for bigger things. His ambition knew no bounds when in 1941 an opportunity came to run for the Senate. He jumped at it without consulting the powers that had put him where he was.

For the first and only time, Texas politics had not included Lyndon Johnson in the big plan. The lesson he had to learn was a sharp one. Governor W. Lee "Pass the Biscuits, Pappy" O'Daniel was running for the Senate. He had nothing to offer the people of Texas in the way of representation except homilies and banjo music. His campaign platform was "The Ten Commandments and the Golden Rule." In keeping with his religious bent, he stood foursquare for prohibition.

Johnson had four years behind him in the House, the support of Roosevelt, and money, money, money to throw into the election. Although $25,000 for a Senate campaign was the spending limit imposed by federal law, Johnson is rumored to have spent half a million dollars. His campaign was financed in part by Herman Brown of Brown and Root Construction Company.

Brown was a conservative, but he was also a businessman to his fingertips. Through his support of the liberal Johnson, he saw his reputation as an independent, self-sufficient entrepreneur evaporate as he fattened on government patronage and became CEO of a huge, collectivized corporate empire. For decades Brown and Root signs were on every large construction project in Texas.

They built huge power plants and dams as part of Roosevelt's Rural Electrification initiative. Housing projects and road construction, of course, were ongoing. But the biggest of all had come from Johnson's membership on the House Naval Affairs Committee. In 1940—through Johnson's lobbying—Brown and Root was awarded the contract to build the Corpus Christi Naval Air Station. It was big! It was huge! Jobs, jobs, jobs. Money, money, money!

With all the "pork" Johnson brought into Texas, he should have been a shoe-in for senator. He spoke to hundreds and thousands of people who cheered as he campaigned from his helicopter "The Johnson City Windmill." Again his health suffered for his efforts to reach out and touch everybody in Texas. And everybody in Texas was impressed.

Nevertheless, he was not supposed to win.

The reason why was political and personal and tainted. It was the brother of the reason why Lyndon was given the post of Kleberg's secretary.

Coke Stevenson, the lieutenant governor, was a friend of the Fergusons. He was also a friend of the beer industry that had supported Jim and Ma in their campaigns. Farmer Jim and Ma wanted "Calculatin' Coke" to be governor of Texas so the sale of beer would be allowed at military bases. This was payback time Texas style, for it was generally known among those who knew such things that the Texas Brewers' Association had contributed $156,000 to Ferguson's campaign for re-election. That particular contribution was part of the reason he was impeached. While Farmer Jim never admitted where the money came from, he believed in paying his debts.

If O'Daniel didn't win the Senate, "The Golden Rule" was going to be the governor. Here the situational irony is inescapable. Johnson was an anti-prohibitionist. O'Daniel was for prohibition, but the anti-prohibition forces wanted him out of Texas. The only way to get him out was to put him in the Senate seat that Johnson wanted.

Too bad for Sam Johnson's boy, but it just wasn't his turn. As John Connally, one of Johnson's closest friends, said, "All of us felt a grave injustice had been done—there was no question about that... But Johnson... was a young man and another election would occur within a year."

On such seemingly small issues do great elections turn.

On June 29 Johnson was declared the winner of the primary by more than five thousand votes with 96 counties counted. On July 1 Jim Ferguson called in the votes from the east and south Texas counties. From Orange, Tyler, Nacogdoches, and Angelina in the Piney Woods, from Duval, Kenedy, and Jim Wells Counties in South Texas came the "corrected totals." They showed O'Daniel had won by 1,311 votes. O'Daniel went to Washington as junior senator. Stevenson went to the governor's mansion.

Sent back to the House of Representatives disappointed and embarrassed, Johnson promised himself, "If I ever get in another close election, I'm not going to lose it."

Back in Washington Roosevelt advised him, "Next time, sit on the ballot boxes."

Winning in the War

On December 7 Pearl Harbor was attacked. On December 8 Johnson had to keep one of this campaign promises. He requested active duty. He boasted that he was the first congressman to do so. Actually, he was lucky to be a representative instead of a junior senator. Since he was a key member of the House Naval Affairs Committee, he could ask for and receive a commission as a lieutenant commander in the Naval Reserve.

He was never patriotic, never actually planned to serve. He viewed the commission as a promise kept to his voters and an opportunity for him to build up political capital for his future career. He did not give up his congressional seat or his place on the committee, but he expected the United States Navy to find a role for him.

The navy had no choice but to do so. He was an officer without military training or aptitude, yet he had power over them because he was a congressional overseer. In keeping with his work ethic, he had not come to play at being a sailor.

The attitude of the navy was that such politicians are trouble, but they are frequently worth whatever it takes to keep them happy because of the influence they wield for military appropriations. From "on high" came orders to spare no expense and make every effort to keep Johnson busy and entertained. Wherever he went, he received all the deference of an admiral.

The Texas press was filled with stories of heroes such as Infantry Lieutenant Audie Murphy from Farmersville and Submarine Commander Sam Dealey from Dallas. They were the most decorated soldier and sailor in the armed services. Admiral Chester Nimitz from Fredericksburg was the commander of the Pacific Fleet.

Recognizing the competition within his state was devastating, Johnson demanded to see action. His reputation depended on it. He was given an assignment in San Francisco, but all he was doing was training navy employers for war production. In May after much lobbying, he received his chance to get near the fighting.

As part of a low-level military team, he was sent to the South Pacific by way of Australia. Like any professional politician, he made good use of the time. He interviewed Douglas MacArthur, toured military bases, and flew north all the way to New Guinea.

In June he insisted on joining his team on a twelve-plane bombing mission over Lae, a Japanese base on the north shore of New Guinea. Johnson missed the takeoff of the B-26 to which he was assigned. Another officer took his place while Johnson, with a borrowed parachute, flew on the second one out. Two dozen Japanese Zeros attacked the squadron. One of the bombers went down in flames.

The Zeros strafed Johnson's plane and knocked out one of the engines. It had to jettison its bombs and turn back for its base. Trailing smoke, it limped home. Zeros in pursuit continued to make strafing runs that tore holes in the fuselage. Against the odds Johnson's plane made it safely back to base with everyone aboard.

The plane he was supposed to take was shot down. Its crew was killed; the other officer died with them. Shocked and grieving, he walked away unscathed and visited wounded men in the Port Moresby hospital shortly thereafter. On a return flight to Melbourne, the B-17 transporting him had to make an emergency landing in the Australian outback. Shaken and exhausted, Johnson, nevertheless, used the opportunity to talk politics with local officials. Whatever derogatory comments can be made about him, he displayed courage under fire and retained his presence of mind to continue being what he was intended to be—a representative of the United States.

On July 1 Roosevelt called him back to Washington. Sam Rayburn had lobbied for the return of the legislature. Congressmen had the option of resigning their seats or returning. Four did resign and remained in service.

Johnson never considered doing so. His "navy career" had convinced him that he was untrained for anything except politics. Furthermore, he was astute enough to know that he was serving no good purpose being transported to different zones by men and machinery that could be put to better use elsewhere.

His dead replacement received the Distinguished Service Cross, and Johnson received a Silver Star. The pilot and crew of his plane, who were just doing their jobs, received no medals or commendations for the flight. Nevertheless, Johnson kept a copy of the commendation in his files and always wore the tiny ribbon that went with the medal. Twenty years later, millions saw without recognizing the tiny white rectangle on his lapel in the famous photograph taken aboard Air Force One with Jacqueline Kennedy on his left and Lady Bird on his right.

Until he returned, Lady Bird did his job as so many wives of men in service were called upon to do. In this case she did for him what he had done for Dick Kleberg. Lonely and swamped by work, she took business courses in the evenings, dealt with Johnson's constituents, and performed all the assignments that Johnson gave her in his daily phone calls. The experience did for her what it had done for Johnson. She developed political savvy as well as courage under pressure.

On his return, Johnson settled into the congressional seat as if he had never left it. He moved in and out of the White House at will. Always liberal in his views and passionately determined to better the lot of the poor farmers and workers, he supported Roosevelt in everything. He formed his own Naval Affairs Subcommittee, which awarded Brown and Root—among others—military contracts around the world.

Yet with all his success, he lacked the fame and popularity he sought. Was he even then looking at the White House, the Oval Office, and the fireside chats with yearning eyes? Even with Roosevelt dying before his eyes, he could not help but envy the presidential "big chair."

By 1943 Lady Bird Johnson had in her hands $36,000 of an inheritance. George Brown gave her stock tips. Charles M. Marsh, the owner of two Austin newspapers, the *Statesman* and the *American*, gave her advice. In 1943 she bought KTBC, a nearly bankrupt radio station. Judge Roy Hofheinz of Houston, one of the most powerful men in Texas, acted as her counsel. For $17,500 she applied for and received FCC authority to operate it. She moved it into new quarters in the Brown Building (George and Herman were everywhere) and spent the rest of her inheritance acquiring new equipment.

The first year, KTBC became, with Johnson's lobbying, a CBS affiliate and broke even. The second year it turned a profit. Johnson would not have cared if it had lost money. Through it he had instant communication with the rest of Texas. He controlled advertising on the station and recommended clients. By the end of the war, the couple's financial troubles were over forever.

Without any competition in the capital of one of the richest states in the union, the radio station became a highly successful enterprise. After the war its value soared into the millions. KTBC was able shortly thereafter to secure the one VHF channel awarded to Austin. It was a virtual monopoly at Johnson's disposal.

The Ambition To Be Great

Sam Rayburn had spent his life in the House of Representatives without anyone ever considering him for a higher job. Johnson had the Speaker before him as an example as well as the early deaths of both his father and his father's brother. He did not see himself as living to be an old man.

Perhaps in a sort of perverse willingness to bring about his self-fulfilling prophecy, he abused his body. He worked long hours, sometimes days at a time with little rest. He smoked heavily, drank too much, and overate. He had no time for an exercise regimen. He was always at his desk or on the campaign trail.

Though everyone acknowledged that he was an able politician, his colleagues—including President Harry S Truman—regarded him as shallow. He was too interested in the power rather than the people. He, in turn, resented their attitude.

In 1949 he would turn forty with what he was sure was two-thirds of his life behind him. A sense of urgency possessed him.

In 1948 after only one term, Pappy O'Daniel decided to quit the Senate. Lyndon Johnson saw the job he was meant to have. But Coke Stevenson, the Texas governor, wanted the O'Daniel seat. For the second time in the decade, Coke and Lyndon faced off in the winner-take-all fight they had fought before. The battle of the heavyweights was about to begin.

"Calculatin'" Coke was a formidable opponent with his governorship the result of Jim Ferguson's political power. But Jim Ferguson was dead. And Miriam held a special grudge against the man who hadn't come to see her husband as he lay on his deathbed.

Moreover, Lyndon had represented Texans, served at least nominally in World War II, and packed ten years of governmental experience behind him. He had powerful friends, and though

Roosevelt was dead, the "feist dog" Harry Truman had taken the reins in his surprisingly competent and strong hands.

Truman was not the supporter that Roosevelt would have been, but Lyndon was extremely important to Truman's own election. Senator Strom Thurmond of South Carolina had taken four southern states and their all-important electoral votes into a party he called the Dixiecrats. In a last-gasp echo of the Civil War, their platform was States' Rights. Truman needed Texas if he was going to defeat Thomas E. Dewey. Therefore, he sent Johnson more than generous money and support.

Still, the campaign was a difficult one for Lyndon because he ran himself so hard that his health again began to deteriorate. More difficult than physical was the politics of trying to please "*all* of the people" at least *some* of the time. Always a liberal at heart, he dared not lose the middle ground where most conservative Texans stood. Although Roosevelt's New Deal had done wonders for the state in terms of Social Security, farm price supports, REA power, and huge amounts of money in the form of appropriations that had gone into deep pockets from the Red River to the Rio Grande, people were suspicious of the way their government was interfering in their lives.

To maintain his position Johnson made no speeches where he pitted one class against the other. Instead, he concentrated on support for Truman's Cold War policies. He repudiated organized labor, welfare measures including health insurance, and ironically civil rights.

He stood foursquare with oil interests by promising to introduce a favorable tax for oil producers and by promising to retain state control over tideland oil, which was just being recognized as the area of the next big boom.

In August 1948, while campaigning by helicopter in as many as ten county seats in a day, he collapsed. Kidney stones racked him with pain. He was forced into the hospital in a state of depression almost as severe as the stones.

Texas Politicians: Good 'n' Bad

Senator Lyndon Johnson campaigns for re-election among ranchers and oilmen at the dedication of a country club in Snyder, Texas.

Again Lady Bird was at his side. He was only forty years old, but he looked sixty. The stones passed. He forced himself up from his bed and went back on the trail as if nothing had happened. But they both knew that he had had a life-threatening incident. He might have stopped then, left the race, and left Washington, but for the very life of him, he could not.

The story of his "landslide" victory is part of Texas legend. Whether Miriam Ferguson actually called George Parr is open to speculation. Johnson was known to have gone to Parr with hat in hand. In Texas then as now, it wasn't what you knew but who you knew that counted. Johnson certainly knew who to go to when he needed to steal an election. He had had one stolen from him by—ironically—Coke Stevenson.

Johnson's statewide margin including the 202 votes from Box 13 was 87 votes.

Of course, Stevenson contested the election. "I was beaten by a stuffed ballot box," he told reporters. "And I can prove it." When he and his lawyers Kellis Dibrell and Jim Gardner, who were former FBI agents, entered George Parr's office in Duval County, Parr laughed in their angry faces. He wasn't an election judge he maintained. He had absolutely nothing to do with the election except to vote, as every good citizen should. He spread his hands, shrugged his shoulders, and showed them the door.

The three went next to Alice in Jim Wells County where Harry Adams had just been elected chairman of the County Democratic Executive Committee. Adams reported that the "amended" total had 203 names added all in the same handwriting, in alphabetical order, and in blue ink.

But the list was in the hands of the outgoing chairman, Tom Donald, an employee of Parr's bank, who had locked it in the bank vault.

Stevenson called for Captain Frank Hamer of the Texas Rangers, famous for shooting the notorious outlaws Bonnie Parker and Clyde Barrow. Hamer came to the bank with Stevenson, Dibrell, and Gardner. As they approached the front door, Hamer motioned several of Parr's armed gunmen to step aside.

Only for the ruthless ranger would they have done so.

Donald let the three men, including the governor of Texas, see the list, but only for a few minutes. He further refused to let it be taken from the bank.

Dibrell and Gardner were able to memorize enough of the list to see that it was indeed in alphabetical order and that at least three of the names on the list belonged to people who had long been dead. They also contacted two other people from the list and obtained their affidavits declaring that they had not voted.

Stevenson set out to force the County Executive Committee to investigate and throw out Box 13.

Johnson obtained a temporary injunction from District Judge Roy C. Archer in Austin, prohibiting the County Committee from investigating because Hamer's presence had been threatening and intimidating.

Stevenson brought the matter before the Democratic Executive Committee and the State Democratic Convention. Twenty-eight delegates voted to throw it out. Twenty-eight delegates voted to keep it.

Johnson pulled a supporter off the Galveston beach. C. C. Gibson of Amarillo charged into the chamber in Fort Worth. "I'm Charley Gibson from Amarillo," he yelled, "and I vote for Lyndon."

By one vote Johnson was allowed to include the vital Box 13 in the vote totals.

Stevenson tried to take the fight to the convention floor the next day, but Johnson formed a coalition with the Truman supporters. Apart they could not win, but together they were in the majority. They voted to expel the anti-Truman and anti-Johnson delegates.

Smiling broadly, Johnson appeared on the platform where he was given a standing ovation. George Parr came up beside him to be introduced and applauded.

Stevenson took his appeal to the Federal Courts on the grounds that half a million Texas voters had been defrauded. U.S. District Judge T. Whitfield Davidson declared, "There has not been one word of evidence submitted to disprove this plaintiff's claim that he has been robbed of a seat in the United States Senate."

He appointed a special commissioner who began an investigation. He was to report back within two weeks. Unfortunately, he learned that a remarkable number of witnesses were vacationing in Mexico, and nowhere could he find copies of the poll lists to determine just what had happened on Election Day.

The case rocked on until November when Johnson beat the Republican candidate by 400,000 votes. Finally, Stevenson was forced to give up.

Most Texans who knew about such things concluded that there was probably no real injustice involved. A close scrutiny of Duval County's previous races would have revealed that Coke Stevenson, then in favor with Ma and Pa Ferguson, had carried George Parr's dukedom by thousands of votes to a mere handful for four successive elections over eight years. What happened to Stevenson was not that he had been *defrauded*, but that he had been *outfrauded*.

Another question asked by those who follow political doings is what the outcome of the election would have been had Stevenson gone to see Pa Ferguson when Ma asked him to.

Johnson grumbled for years that Box 13 wasn't the election. It was just the nomination. And so it was, but in Texas, a one-party state that belonged lock, stock, and barrel to the Democrats, the primary was the all-important vote.

One unforgettable story out of the debacle must have pierced Johnson to the quick. Though he had a sense of humor, he hated to be the butt of any joke. This one circulated throughout Texas and made its way into the marble halls of Washington, D.C.

> A little Mexican boy was sitting on a curbstone in Alice, Texas, weeping his heart out.
>
> A friend discovered him and asked what was wrong.
>
> "*Mi padre. Mi padre,*" Juanito sobbed. "He was here last Saturday, but he no come to see me."
>
> The friend was amazed. "But, Juanito, your father's been dead for three years."

"*Sí,*" the little boy wept. "*Es verdad.* But they told me he was here last Saturday to vote for Lyndon Johnson—and he no come to see me."

The Bit in His Teeth

In 1949 Johnson moved from the House to the Senate. Immediately he began "politicking" with a vengeance. With Lady Bird smiling at his side, he courted and became friends with the most able people in the Senate. He sought positions on influential committees, and the leaders, taking advice from Sam Rayburn, gave him the positions that he sought.

In 1951 he became the Senate Majority Whip. In 1953 he was the Senate Minority Leader, and in 1955, the Senate Majority Leader. Never had a senator risen so rapidly. Never would a leader so dominate the Senate as Johnson did over the next five years.

Richard Russell, the most powerful Democrat in the Senate, in particular was targeted by Lyndon as the man who could do him the most good. He and Lady Bird adopted Russell as they had Rayburn. Both men were bachelors who were delighted to be invited into a young couple's home on a regular basis. Besides his ingrained Texas respect for his elders, Lady Bird and daughters Lynda and Luci were Johnson's greatest asset in this warm, friendly setting.

Russell for his part used Johnson to do the hard work of coalition building. The junior senator was willing, ready, and extremely able. Since he hardly ever slept, he used the telephone until all hours of the night, molding opinions and shaping alliances. He identified the people who had clout, those who were respected and effective, and made himself valuable to them. Soon Johnson was actually making all the basic decisions, but he maintained the fiction that Russell and his cronies were

Lyndon Baines Johnson

LBJ in action against Abe Fortas, one of Johnson's most trusted advisors. Johnson used the up-close and very personal body argument on allies and foes.
LBJ Library Photo Archives

the initiators of the legislation and that he simply carried out their wishes.

The new kid on the block had courted and flattered his way into the gang, and before anyone knew it, he'd taken over. For two years no one knew he was around, except the men he worked with, who thought he was working for them.

By 1953 he had settled into the traces. In that year he bought the old Johnson homeplace on the Pedernales and the Martin ranch up the way. Together he and Lady Bird created the LBJ Ranch, their dream home where he entertained and charmed guests who came away prepared to aid him politically. Born like most Texans with a love of the land, Johnson never loved anything so much as he loved that ranch. Immediately he adopted the Western persona of cowboy boots and Western hats. He counted every cow and horse, hunted deer and turkey in the fall, rode and drove across the land as if he were to the "saddle" born.

It was his fantasy and his escape. It symbolized the honest, simple life that he had never lived. It was romantic in the way that the entire West was being romanticized in films and romantic fiction. He became part of the landed gentry with Richard Russell of Georgia, Clinton Anderson of New Mexico, and Robert Kerr of Oklahoma. Together they stood in the Senate cloakroom, talked "ranch talk," and devised legislation that would shape the world.

By this time he had also settled into a greater role for himself. He no longer thought of himself as a simple representative from Texas. He thought of himself as shaping a nation. From the cloakroom came national policies and strategies that affected the entire forty-eight states.

During 1955 he made a special trip home to Texas to honor one of the people whom rumor and legend credits with the beginning of his meteoric rise to fame. The trip underscores what his enemies (of whom he had many) knew and frequently had cause to regret.

Senator Lyndon Johnson never forgot a political slight *or* a political favor. On June 13, 1955, more than three hundred Texas Democrats gathered at the Driskill in Austin to celebrate Miriam Ferguson's eightieth birthday.

The Senate Majority Leader made the congratulatory address. He lauded the Fergusons as politicians "who stand for the folks—four-square and without apology and no compromise.

"Governor," he said to the smiling lady, "I traveled 1,600 miles to be with you tonight, and I would gladly travel 1,600 more."

In light of what she and Farmer Jim had done for him, his statement was totally appropriate. In light of what he had done and was to do for Texas, the gift from her friends, a beautiful gold bracelet watch engraved with the numerals "80," was a fitting token of their appreciation.

As Senate Majority Leader, he was one of the most important and well-known men in the United States. He was also a chain-smoking, food-shoveling workaholic who literally leaned on people when he talked to them, overpowering them with his height, his voice, and his energy.

Had he not had a heart attack the same year, few doubted that he would have been a presidential candidate in 1956. He was only forty-eight years old, but he had driven himself so hard that the attack was severe. He actually contemplated quitting politics forever.

His friends in the Senate and his constituents refused to hear of it. They knew as surely as the dawning of a new era that the next president would not be a man born in the nineteenth century. Instead, he would be a young man. Johnson stood a good chance to be that man. By following a careful regimen and resting, he could live on and prosper. Johnson must stay.

They promised his turn would come.

With those promises to bolster his spirits, Johnson plunged into his role of Senate Majority Leader with a "body count" mentality. Every piece of legislation was weighed in terms of how many people could be counted on to vote for it. How could it be modified to bring others on board? How many supporters would it lose if certain items were dropped?

Many despised him as a hypocrite and an opportunist. Many of those were in his native state. He characterized himself as reasonable and rational. In the article "My Political Philosophy" for the *Texas Quarterly*, he classified himself among other things as a liberal, a conservative, a Texan, a taxpayer, and a voter. He argued that "a national answer exists for every national question" thereby implying that he served all Americans.

The president might change from Democrat to Republican, as Truman was replaced by Dwight D. Eisenhower, but Lyndon Johnson remained to serve the office—not the man.

In the fifties most citizens had little idea how a bill came to a vote. They never understood that major legislation required years, sometimes decades to produce. Various constituencies had to be appeased and appealed to. Every congressman votes for a different bill—his parts, which are the parts that he can take home and use to gain re-election. The parts that are the most statesmanlike, those that create the greatest good for the greatest number of people, are frequently downplayed or ignored when the representative presents it to his voters.

Therefore, elements of deceit are built into the writing, and bills pass because of *selective emphasis* and *selective concealment*.

Johnson worked hard to get out the vote for the highway bill by which the interstate system was born. Even though the appropriations would continue for decades, he was able to get a key piece removed that required union wages on all construction. Although the bill would provide jobs for thousands of men all across the country, organized labor hated him for that one provision. While the southern states, where unions were few and far between, hated the ideas of the taxes that the system would cost, they approved of him because he saved their money.

He guided the Senate through the explosion of communist fears generated by Senator Joseph McCarthy, whose hearings to roust out communism in America are—to this day—considered a shame and a disgrace to the ideals of freedom.

Johnson led the Senate to vote 75-12 to appoint a committee to investigate the rabid senator's behavior. He then selected the elder statesmen for the committee—John Stennis, Edwin Johnson, and Sam Ervin—perfect for the job with judicial training and strong conservative stances. The appointments created an air of unity, with Johnson taking the position that the inquiry must not be a party thing. And in the end it was not. The motion of censure demonstrated to all who paid attention to politics that Johnson was master of the highest legislative body in the land.

Political crazies in Texas hated him for his opposition to McCarthy. They demanded that Johnson stand foursquare against communism. His Texan voting base remained loyal, but many were becoming disillusioned. Was a vote against McCarthy a vote *for* communism?

With Sputnik, the tiny Russian satellite, beeping its way around earth, as chairman of the Preparedness Subcommittee, Johnson used his political expertise, his network for analysis of the situation, and his growing eminence to investigate the "missile gap." When he presented his recommendations on the floor, the result was possibly the most important piece of legislation to bear his name. He created the National Aeronautics and Space Administration. Of course, being Johnson, he made certain that its headquarters were in Houston.

He led the fight for the Civil Rights Act of 1957 although he had always stood against civil rights legislation. It had originated with the Eisenhower Republicans, who saw it as a means of splitting the Democratic Party. What it sought to do was to provide equal justice under the law for people accused of civil contempt.

In its substantive effect, it provided protection for black voting rights by making civil rights protests a matter of civil rather than criminal contempt. Jury trials were necessary only in civil cases. Judges could decide in criminal cases. Placing civil rights in the hands of twelve rather than one, Johnson told his constituents, was reasonable.

Further protection was provided to help people in the South devise machinery to solve the problems of school desegregation so long as the protests were civil. It provided for a civil rights commission and established a civil rights division in the Justice Department.

In the end he led the floor fight although all the votes were already in place. His and others' posturing and speechmaking were necessary for the press and the voters. While the bill was not what Eisenhower wanted, he reluctantly signed it.

Johnson breathed a sigh of relief. He knew tougher, more specific bills were to come, seeking federal aid to education, medical care for the aged, public housing, and increased minimum wages. For him the bill was a brilliant success. He had gained enormous publicity for accomplishing the impossible—the passage of the first civil rights bill since Reconstruction.

In 1960 the senator from Massachusetts tapped him for the vice-presidency. Both were entering the race with major handicaps. Kennedy was a Roman Catholic—the object of much religious prejudice. Johnson was a Southerner—the object of much regional prejudice.

Many stories have been told about why he accepted the nomination. Probably the reality is that he regarded it as a step above the Senate Majority Leader. "One heartbeat from the presidency." The ambitious country boy from the Pedernales was always climbing higher on the ladder. Even though

Theodore Roosevelt had wept when he was forced to take the vice-presidency, Johnson believed he could do more than Roosevelt had done.

He believed he could become more.

The New Job

Johnson always leaped at opportunities to accept new challenges. The idea of the vice-presidency energized him, drove him to work harder and longer, to achieve more and more. He could not turn the job down, because if he did he would never be considered again. Throughout Kennedy's short three years in office, Johnson's loyalty was never in question, although his temper and his patience were sorely tried.

Kennedy was the boss, the chief, the leader. Johnson recognized his position and honored the president. In so doing, he made a great personality shift. He hated the new role because from leader of the Senate he became a servant to the real power.

He was able to be the "best one that had ever been" because his entire career in politics had been one of compromise. He was determined to be the "champion vice president of all time" because to be less would to be a failure and above all he hated failure, feared it, and was embarrassed by it. For those reasons he strove preternaturally to avoid it and to put himself on the winning side in all things. Ironically, his weakness of character was the source of his strength.

He knew his presence had not benefited the ticket as much as he would have liked. His speeches seeking to bind together North and South, black and white, Protestant and Catholic were not well received. Ironically, the most votes for the ticket were the sympathy votes garnered by an incident at the venerable Adolphus Hotel in Dallas.

LBJ and Lady Bird were harassed and actually assaulted by right-wing fanatics. As they climbed from their car, the crowd shouted insults and waved placards in their faces. Several of the women rushed forward to push Lady Bird and pull her hair. Steely-eyed in the face of such treatment, Johnson assumed the impassive demeanor of judge as he assisted his frightened wife inside. It took them half an hour to cross the lobby. The *Dallas Morning News* took pictures that made the front pages, and the national wire services picked up the story.

Southerners all across the South were extremely embarrassed. Liberals thought the incident meant that Johnson had joined their camp. Americans are by and large a gentle, civil people. To Texas men, who voted in record numbers, the assault on a lady was unforgivable. The rudeness and violence of that morning may actually have given Texas to the Democrats.

Once in the White House, Johnson felt acutely embarrassed and inferior to Kennedy, whose education he knew he lacked. The farm boy from Texas had never been fashionable, had a third-rate education, cared nothing for art, and was plebeian in his taste. When Pablo Casals played the cello at the White House, Johnson did not understand what he was listening to.

Actually, Kennedy knew very little more than Johnson did about what he was listening to, but he managed to preserve the fiction that he, who had been reared with a silver spoon in his mouth, had a deep and abiding love of music and the arts.

Johnson thought that Kennedy had filled the place with intellectuals, among whom he felt off balance. He was mistaken, but he had neither the experience nor the talent to detect the superficiality of Camelot, as Kennedy's administration came to be called. For the first time city slickers had buffaloed the country boy. Ironically, no less a prestigious paper than *The Wall Street Journal* in 2001 would call Johnson "one of the three most intellectually interesting presidents of the past forty years."

He was even jealous of Kennedy's wife, Jacqueline, who at thirty-one was as alien in the White House as he was. His own Lady Bird, who had made substantial gains in her social graces and would gain many more, seemed dull and uninteresting by contrast.

The reverse was actually true. While John Kennedy had married an ornament for his arm, Johnson's wife was his indispensable advisor. She protected his character and his ego. She kept herself informed on the issues and was cagey in dealing with people who might hurt him or try to take advantage of him. She had substance, strength of character, grace, and compassion. By comparison, Jacqueline Kennedy had a long way to go.

One thing Johnson did know was that he was much better prepared to be president than Kennedy. This knowledge sustained him and drove him to make the most of his job. As Kennedy's legislative program floundered, Johnson knew he was pulling in double harness with a rank amateur who might be able to function in a Harvard classroom but didn't have a clue as to how to make government work.

With that certainty in his mind, he sought to bring life to his office. First, Johnson asked to retain his position as chair of the Democratic caucus. He was disappointed when his former colleagues reminded him he was no longer a legislator but an executive.

No one knows whether Johnson reminded Kennedy of his promise to give Johnson a position in government. What is known is that very soon in his presidency, Kennedy created the President's Committee on Equal Employment. In 1964 with the reins in his hands, Johnson turned it into the Equal Employment Opportunities Commission—one of the most enduring federal efforts on behalf of working people.

Would the EEOC have been so important without Johnson at its head? Would it have lasted so long?

Under Johnson its membership included all heads of the Departments of the Interior, Labor, Commerce, and Defense as well as the Civil Service Agency, NASA, the Bureau of the Budget, and the General Services Administration. Certainly, Kennedy never envisioned such a powerhouse as his vice president turned it into.

Johnson quickly recommended a monumental "affirmative step." It required provisions in every government contract to forbid discrimination because of race, creed, color, or national origin. Each agency head, or contractor, was required to take "affirmative action" to fulfill this goal in the areas of recruitment, employment, promotions, transfers, layoffs, raises, and selections for training.

It was monumental! It was sweeping! No one recognized it for what it was. No one could know, but it was the beginning of the Johnson presidency!

To set the tone in 1962, Johnson hired a black lawyer, Hobart Taylor Jr., a Texan by birth, to implement the Plan for Progress among cooperating firms. Together Johnson and Taylor launched a crusade on behalf of nondiscrimination.

The future society of the United States was being shaped. When 104 firms joined the Plan for Progress, Johnson set out to bring everyone in. It was something he could do. He could persuade, he could cajole, he could threaten. He was good at it.

Ironically, he who had been elected originally as an ultra-conservative from an ultra-conservative state had become passionately committed to civil rights. His initiatives and the publicity they gained led to lunch counter sit-ins, freedom rides, and finally Martin Luther King's huge march on Washington in 1963.

The racial issue had become the greatest challenge to the United States and its political system. The talented and savvy Johnson had spent his lifetime solving problems. He loved the challenges. He had led himself into the light again. He had a special responsibility to make all the people in the United States happy. Gain a consensus, gain justice, and do it with as little conflict as possible.

How it must have galled him to know he could not do it himself! All his work would be credited to Kennedy's administration. Still, he never faltered in his role of mentor and advisor. With everything in place he called Ted Sorenson, Kennedy's special counsel and speechwriter. In a conversation recorded on a cassette is one of the most selfless political moves ever known. Sorenson offered no interruptions except an occasional "yes, sir," as Johnson told the youngster how the young president must do it:

If Kennedy wanted the impending civil rights bill passed, he must pace himself. Timing was everything. First, get Congress to pass a tax cut that would please the people and ensure re-election, then bring out the big guns for civil rights. Open with a great speech in Mississippi to establish the moral high ground and drive the bigots into a hole. Place the whole thing on a moral tone.

Kennedy, he continued, must put the majority of the country squarely behind the blacks. He reminded Sorenson of Johnson's own speech at Gettysburg in the spring of 1963. "One hundred years ago, the slave was freed. One hundred years later, the Negro remains in bondage to the color of his skin."

He suggested that Kennedy make a speech very much like that in San Antonio, where Texans could hear it and mass behind him.

Shortly thereafter, Johnson was included in the planning of a special presidential trip to Texas. Some sources say that the trip amounted to a vote of confidence from Kennedy to Johnson. Others have always maintained that the presence of John and Nellie Connally in the car with Kennedy was a statement that

Texas Politicians: Good 'n' Bad

The most famous photograph in the world.
Note the ribbon for the Silver Star that LBJ wears in his lapel.
Judge Sarah T. Hughes administered the oath November 22, 1963.
LBJ Library Photo Archives

Johnson was out. Whatever the truth, fate relegated him to the fourth car back.

At about 12:30 P.M., the presidential car turned onto the downhill slope of Elm Street from the old red courthouse. Crowds lined the grass and the sidewalk on either side. The Texas Schoolbook Depository loomed above it. People standing in its windows had a clear view down into the car.

Three rifle shots rang out in quick succession. One so shattered Kennedy's brain as to leave him legally dead. Connally was also badly wounded.

One horrific piece of film shows Jacqueline crawling across the back of the car to pull the Secret Service man in on top of her while in the front seat beside the driver, Nellie covers John with her body. The limousine driver stomps on the gas and speeds down through the triple underpass toward Parkland Hospital.

Back in Johnson's car, which had not entered the street, a Secret Service man had already covered Johnson's body with his own. In that moment Johnson had no idea that he had inherited the duties of the president of the United States.

At 2:40 P.M., with Lady Bird on Johnson's right and Jacqueline on his left, Judge Sarah T. Hughes administered the oath of office on board Air Force One.

In one horrifying stroke Johnson had all he desired, but he was at heart a simple patriot. He loved Texas and he loved America. What had happened to Kennedy assaulted all Americans and their institutions.

At the pinnacle of his power, he did not know whether he was equal to the task. The awful experience humbled him as nothing else ever had. Like Truman after the death of Roosevelt, Johnson had no time to ponder. Like a soldier, he plunged back into the work that lay before him—to pass Kennedy's bill.

Before Congress he said, "All I have I would have gladly given not to be standing here today."

And during the service at St. Mark's Episcopal Church the next Sunday, he wept.

The Pinnacle of Power

Seven weeks later he delivered his State of the Union message to the joint houses of Congress. His words rang with conviction. "This administration today, here and now, declares unconditional war on poverty in America." He pledged to end American racism, which he called a moral issue. He named his vision of an America without color, with equal opportunity for all, as "The Great Society."

In that speech he put in motion an army of men and women who came to Washington to erect its offices. The whole thing was anathema to conservatives. But no one who was involved in it in those years could miss the energy that Johnson generated up and down the country as the people listened and watched and read. Discussions raged from the daises of political power, from the television screens, and from the pages of the newspapers.

It was the beginning of America's crusade for salvation by government.

Lyndon Johnson had never stood so far from the banks of the Pedernales, from his nondescript education, from his self-serving, opportunistic persona as he did at that moment. He had become that most dangerous of men—the idealist with the power to achieve his ideals.

As might have been expected, he threw himself into the task as only he could. Both barrels blazing, he exploded through the ranks of Congress, doling out public works projects, prized appointments, photo opportunities. His colleagues saw him as the 800-pound gorilla prowling where he wanted to. No one dared to argue with him.

He was on the phone night after night, day after day. Conducting business in his pajamas from his bed, he called individual senators. "A president is a political leader," he said, "and he can never be above politics." He worked at a frantic pace, sleeping only three or four hours a night.

A story was told that he called one of his trusted advisors at 3:00 A.M. "Were you asleep?" he barked into the phone.

"Oh, no, Mr. President," the man replied. "I was just lying here waiting for your call."

He kept the House in session until the night before Christmas to pass a foreign aid bill to allow credits to the Soviet Union to purchase American grain. Then he pitched a gala Christmas party to appease their outrage. In only one month he gained complete control of Washington as few presidents achieve in their first year.

He and Lady Bird flew home to the LBJ ranch the next day. His huge Cadillac was there to meet them at the Austin airport. Instead of letting the Secret Service man drive, he put his bodyguards in the backseat and the accelerator to the floorboard.

People saw him streaking down Highway 290 toward Johnson City. A joke circulated.

> A trooper saw a huge Cadillac rocket by him. He turned on his siren and sped in pursuit. Several miles later, it pulled to a halt.
>
> The trooper climbed off the motorcycle and came to the window. He found himself staring into Lyndon Johnson's angry face.
>
> "My God," he whispered.
>
> Lady Bird leaned forward and nodded. "And don't you forget it, young man."

Back in Washington in January 1964, Johnson launched his first crusade for the new legislation to create the Great Society. Out of the congressional session came some twenty major bills including the Economic Opportunities Act and a critical tax cut.

To create so much legislation, Johnson inserted himself into every phase of the process, including seeking and getting the cooperation of congressmen who became his key advisors. A superb political animal, he wined and dined them, made them feel appreciated and flattered. They voted as he wanted.

To satisfy a disturbed country where more and more outrageous rumors circulated every day, he bullied Chief Justice Earl Warren into heading a commission that would bear his name. Its purpose was to investigate every phase of the assassination of his predecessor. In addition, Johnson named the most respected men in the Congress to serve on it including his friend Richard Russell.

"I can't arrest you," he bellowed over the phone when Russell tried to demur, "and I'm not going to put the FBI on you, but you're goddam sure going to serve. I'll tell you that."

While business continued at a frantic pace in Washington, the conflict in Vietnam was fast turning into an undeclared war. He was desperate to conceal it from the American people and from Congress until he could get his legislation passed. As commander in chief he escalated it secretly, while he provided Congress with overly optimistic military reports. The situation grew worse and worse. Casualties reached 500 a week. It divided the country and undoubtedly led to the demonstrations and turmoil of the seventies.

How well he succeeded in his drive to pull the country behind him to accomplish his goals and how well he succeeded in deceiving the country are measured by the election results of 1964. His first and only time to run for the presidency of the United States, Johnson won over sixty-one percent of the popular vote and the largest plurality in history. His opponent Barry Goldwater won only his home state Arizona and the states in the Deep South, still adamantly opposed to any civil rights for blacks.

To assess and discuss the incredible amount of legislation that Johnson managed to extract from the Congress after that kind of mandate would require many more pages than this

Lyndon Baines Johnson

At their beloved ranch on Election Day, 1964, LBJ and Lady Bird await the news that he will be elected the thirty-sixth president of the United States. *Center for American History, UT-Austin*

author has at her disposal. Before the Democrats lost control of Congress in the 1966 elections, *two hundred major bills* were passed and *a dozen landmark measures*. The amount of work enacted was four times the amount Roosevelt was able to manage to bring America out of the depression of 1929.

The center of it all was Lyndon Baines Johnson. He was the progenitor of it all. Working almost twenty-four hours a day seven days most weeks, he made the needed staff assignments, recruited the outside experts, approved a legislative agenda for each session of Congress, and finally set up the administrative machinery to effect all the new programs.

How could one human being do so much in a twenty-four-hour day?

Johnson had two work habits that governed his presidential performance just as they governed his life. First, he could give intense concentration to a task at hand to the exclusion of everything else including his own physical needs. Second, he was possessed of enormous energy to sustain himself through his twenty-hour workday.

In fact, he almost killed himself with all the work. He wanted to achieve all his goals, to perfect every institution, to solve all the problems, to eliminate all the glaring inequalities and injustices. Ever in his great chest, his heart thumped and fluttered, reminding him that he had only a few years to be the president and that he was not going to live long. He had the power. This was the moment. He was determined to make it his own.

In the end he created mistrust among his constituents, among the people he worked with, and particularly among the news people, whom he did not trust. He was never comfortable with them. He hated to speak extemporaneously to the press corps. He tried to manipulate data. He tried impromptu press conferences. He made mistakes. He tried to embellish the truth until statements and stories began to look like lies.

The press and, through them, the public came to believe that Johnson was not only secretive, but extremely duplicitous. A picture appeared across the nation of Lyndon with his eyes slitted, looking upward from under his furrowed brows. The caption read, "Would you buy a used car from this man?"

A highly critical paperback appeared in 1964, *A Texan Looks at Lyndon*. Its message was clear. If his own people can't trust him, who can?

He grew more and more unhappy and more and more morose. By 1967 he was conducting a virtual cold war with the press.

Not With a Bang

By March 1968, 25,000 Americans had lost their lives in Vietnam, less than half the eventual total. The financial costs, already unacceptably high, eventually reached $100 billion.

Johnson was an old man at the age of sixty. He looked it in every line of his great furrowed face. He was experiencing depression, paranoia, and conspiratorial fantasies. His body was a wreck—overweight, under exercised, suffering from the abuses of lack of sleep and proper rest.

He discussed a momentous decision with his closest confidant. Lady Bird agreed whole-heartedly. In fact, she helped him write his speech. On March 31, 1968, he spoke to the nation. Toward the end, he glanced in her direction. She remained smiling and gently sympathetic.

Then he looked directly into the television camera as Harry Truman had done twenty years before. "I shall not seek, and will not accept, the nomination of my party for another term as your president." His excuse was that he needed to devote every hour of the remainder of his term to peace, to bringing home "America's sons in the fields far away," to finishing the work he had begun to heal the "division in the American house."

While that was true, in a sense he surrendered his life. He had reached the pinnacle. He had nowhere else to go except home. There was no new task, no new challenge, no new ambition. Nothing less than a massive public demand could have made him reverse his decision. It never came.

How that must have hurt him!

He had sincerely and magnanimously sacrificed his career for the cause of peace. How could the people he had worked so hard to benefit accept his decision with such equanimity?

He had to face the fact that they wanted him out of their lives.

For ten months he strove to end the war and preserve what he had wrought. The nation paid little attention, for the limelight was drawn elsewhere. Two popular and beloved of its sons, Robert Kennedy and Martin Luther King Jr., were assassinated within months of each other.

At the end of his term, Johnson retired to the ranch with Lady Bird. Acknowledging their debt to him, the Republican administration treated him deferentially. Nixon kept him informed of foreign policy. Henry Kissinger visited him with information and updates.

On December 12, 1972, he hosted an LBJ Library symposium on civil rights. At the end of the evening, he delivered a twenty-minute speech that taxed the strength of his dying body. At one point he had to pause to slip a nitroglycerine tablet under his tongue. Then he called upon the crowd saying, "We have proved that great progress is possible. We know how much still remains to be done. And if our efforts continue, if our will is strong, if our hearts are right, and if courage remains our constant companion, then, my fellow Americans, I am confident that *we shall overcome.*"

Lyndon Baines Johnson

Shortly before his death, LBJ talked with U.S. Representative Barbara Jordan of Texas and NAACP official Vernon Jordan at a symposium on civil rights. Vernon Jordan's reputation was later tarnished by a brush of scandal in the Monica Lewinsky affair with President Bill Clinton during his second term.
LBJ Library Photo Archives

On January 22, 1973, Lady Bird went into Austin. At 3:50 P.M. Johnson suffered his final coronary. He was able to call the ranch switchboard but died before the Secret Service guards got to him.

In Washington, D.C., the same black horse that had followed Kennedy's caisson curveted restlessly behind Johnson's.

He was buried in the family plot beside his grandparents and his parents, safe at home on the banks of the Pedernales.

History's Assessment

Few people loved Lyndon Johnson. His passing was not marked by the adulation that crowds expressed for the slain Kennedy brothers or for Martin Luther King Jr., whose cause he helped so much. Most people read the headline and turned to the sports page.

Irony is the keyword to describe his life. Few people really understand irony. His own restless desire for achievement, his own lack of self-esteem drove him to try to do good wherever he served. Ethicists would call those the wrong reasons. Furthermore, by duplicity, manipulation, and all the qualities that society labels as bad, he did good things. Again ethicists would quarrel with his methods.

What was the nature of the man?

Many will speculate. Perhaps not enough time has passed since he left us. None of his accomplishments has stood the test of time.

But when will that be?

Many of his most important accomplishments as president are still a part of our lives even in the twenty-first century.

Part II

Hot Oil

Taming the Wild Beast

"It's my oil, and if I want to drink it, that's none of your damn business."

Independent oilman Tom G. Patten's remark pretty much reflected the attitude of the majority of Texas in 1931. The idea that what a man did on his own land was his own business and what his land produced—cotton, cattle, or oil—could be sold by him on the open market for whatever price he chose to accept. The boundless acres of Texas and the United States were responsible for the profligate spirit that marked the westward expansion in the first century of the country's growth.

But the pioneers had reached California and Oregon eighty years before. A new era had dawned in which wise Americans saw that preservation of natural resources was going to be this country's responsibility if the land was going to support her children and grandchildren.

At the time of its discovery in America, oil grew from a nuisance to an alternative fuel of limited practicality. Beyond that, it rose in the minds of entrepreneurial men to a valuable resource and a source of wealth beyond their wildest dreams. They thought that it would be with them forever. There was so much of it, gushing into the skies, and what might be its uses was anybody's guess.

Today it has assumed the status of virtual necessity for the entire world. Adding to its value is the fact that the world has come to recognize that it is recoverable *but not* renewable. For all practical purposes the oil flowing and pooling in seams between layers of rock and sand thousands of feet below the earth's crust is all that will ever be.

It is a finite source of power that has already become increasingly difficult to obtain. Once men worked in the pleasant fields of Texas and California where they could be with their families when their tours were done. Now they toil in the killing heat of vast deserts in Saudi Arabia, on steel platforms raised high into the howling winds above the turbulent waters of the North Sea, and on shelves of ice north of the Arctic Circle in Alaska.

Once it made wildcatters into millionaires almost overnight and built Houston, Dallas, and Fort Worth into centers of incredible wealth and power. Now the wildcatters are out of business because oil requires the resources of huge corporations to locate and sink a well. Drilling for oil today involves danger, privation, frightening expense, and more often than not disappointment. While CEOs get stock options, the profits are dispersed among millions of stockholders all over the world.

For oil is a secretive, deceptive resource.

It is much more secretive than gold or coal or uranium. They are solids, which have shape and volume. The space they occupy will not change unless man or some force of nature changes them. Once discovered, they do not move from their position in the mountainside or the pit until they are mined.

Oil is a liquid. While it has volume, it assumes the shape of its container, usually a seam in the earth between two layers of rock or sand or in a basin of sedimentary rock that was once the bed of a prehistoric sea. Herein lies the problem. The seams and basins in the earth do not run vertically like the wells men drill. They run horizontally as pools or—in the case of many Texas fields—lakes.

As a portion of the oil is removed, the rest is forced by the pressure of the associated gas to flow into the vacuum and maintain itself at a more shallow level. At this point the depth of the lake that may extend under the properties of many individuals is decreased. The edges of the lake recede. Gradually, ninety to ninety-five percent of the oil in the lake can be drained because the associated gas has also been trapped under great pressure. It expands as the oil is brought to the surface through the pipe sunk thousands of feet into the earth.

When oil was first drilled in Titusville, Pennsylvania, in 1857, no laws of any sort governed it. Its potential was unknown; its nature had yet to be discovered. No laws assigned ownership. As a result, almost immediately people began to dispute their rights with others. Judges, therefore, looked for analogies with other substances that they *suspected* might have common characteristics.

English common law seemed to provide the answer. Water was a liquid as was oil. It had long been governed by riparian rights. The judges therefore studied riparian, the rights of people whose land abutted a flowing stream. Riparian held that all owners had equal rights to the water which they could use as they desired, *so long* as they did not diminish their neighbors' corresponding rights.

From the onset, unfortunately, riparian did not appear to work because no one truly knew the path or the extent of the oil under the ground. Landowners objected strenuously to that decision. They argued that oil and gas were minerals not water. They countered with their own English common law that recognized a man's absolute dominion over everything above and below his landed estate, including the underlying mineral rights. Oil and gas, therefore, belonged to the man on whose land the well was drilled, not others who happened to be downstream from that oil.

But did they?

When geologists discovered that oil and gas spread throughout horizontal seams, owners asked what was to prevent a well being drilled on the land adjacent to the lease and the oil beneath being drained off.

In the end the courts found another parallel, which remains one of the strangest of modern jurisprudence. They ruled that petroleum was a fugitive. Oil and gas were named *ferae naturae*. Wild animals. Fences and other such ordinary boundaries could not hold them. They had the power to escape without the volition of the owner.

Furthermore, owners were quick to discover or figure out for themselves that if others drilled close to their land, the *ferae naturae* might escape from under them, running out through their neighbor's wellheads and leaving them with dry holes.

The courts ruled that oil and gas were unamenable to legal precedents governing property rights in solid minerals. They therefore fashioned a new rule. Without knowing anything of the science of the resources or what impact their ruling would have on the infant industry, the courts held that oil and gas belonged to the owner of the land. However, they were subject to his control only so long as they remained there. When the oil and gas escaped into other lands, the former owner lost his title.

In other words possession was not nine-tenths of the law. It was *all* of the law—of the jungle. The faster a man could drill, the more oil would be in his possession. Never mind that the oil was exhausted much sooner. Never mind that much of it was wasted when the well was not allowed to "rest" and the associated gas was not allowed to repressurize the seam.

With that rule the Pennsylvania Court turned the oil and gas business into a race that for almost a century wasted millions of barrels of one of the world's most precious resources. Oil was a wild animal. And like many of the wild animals inhabiting the North American continent, it was hunted almost to the point of extinction.

The men who drilled for it became wild animals as well. Drilling night and day, burning off the associated gas when they encountered it, allowing gushers to blow for days without capping them, and pumping the oil out of the ground as fast as they could while leaving as much as eighty-five percent of it behind unrecoverable. No act was too greedy or stupid if it would prevent other men from having one drop of the oil they believed they alone were entitled to.

The result: Dozens of derricks bloomed side by side in the space of a few city blocks as the leaseholders drilled and drilled. Sometimes wells came in gushing oil nearly side by side, the oil pouring forth, obviously from the same source but belonging to two different people.

It was a stupid ruling based on ancient laws and bad science. Even after it had been revealed as stupid, judges continued to be guided by it in rulings that would have destroyed a lesser industry.

* * *

The courts cannot be allowed to bear the full onus of blame. By failing to police itself, the oil industry was to an equal extent responsible for its own problems. In the beginning, overproduction was considered to be a good thing because the extent of oil's possibilities were not known. The capture theory was the easiest way to protect private property interests in a manner that encouraged production. It also fit the theme of law promoting economic development. No real uses existed for oil except as a heating fuel. The internal combustion engine and the automobile were vague drawings in the hands of eccentric inventors.

Oil and gas might or might not be important. They might or might not be worth money. So where was the harm if some was wasted?

In the end Texas paid for the stupidity of others. The history that follows is a tragic example of waste and greed aided and abetted by politicians who failed to act with sanity and dispatch for the benefit of all Texans.

As Captain Anthony Lucas remarked when he surveyed the ruins of the field his drillers' discovery had founded, "The cow was milked too hard, and moreover, she was not milked intelligently."

"The Great Regulator"

James Stephen Hogg

"We intend to have a commission to fix rates, and the railway companies had just as well submit to it. I say Texas will have it! She will regulate the railroads and not be regulated by them."

Taming the Captains of Industry

If ever a man was born to tame a wild animal, he was James Stephen Hogg, the first governor of Texas actually born in the state. Of Scottish ancestry, his name, which meant a young sheep, should have been pronounced to rhyme with the *o* in "noble." However, Texans always pronounced it to rhyme with "hog." His detractors and political opponents often mocked and slandered him with references to greed, size, intemperance, and filth.

Born in Cherokee County in 1851 and orphaned in 1862, he grew to be six-foot-three or four with huge muscular arms and big hands. At eighteen he helped the Wood County sheriff arrest a man who later came with a gang of thugs and shot Hogg in the back. The bullet lodged near his spine. The gang believed Hogg was as good as dead and fled without finishing the job. Possessed of a will to live and inspired by the memory of his father, who had also been shot and survived, he absolutely refused to die. Despite a raging fever and an incompetent doctor who probed and probed with a sharpened pine stick without being able to remove the bullet, Hogg survived.

Despite the terrible pain, he demanded that friends move him out of Wood County, where he was certain his enemies would try again when they heard he was still alive.

While he convalesced, he began reading for the law. In those days a man could actually become a lawyer by reading all the law books he could lay his hands on and passing an examination. As Hogg taught himself, he reported and wrote for the various newspapers in the area. At twenty-two he was elected justice of the peace and was admitted to the bar shortly thereafter. He later became the Wood County attorney.

Many years later, bothered by recurring pain in his back, he called a doctor to the executive mansion in Austin and ordered him to remove the bullet. The doctor did so and sewed the wound up. Hogg returned to work that afternoon.

He was enormously popular with Texas men (with the exception of a few in Cherokee County) among whom he loomed like a great tree. By this time he weighed over three hundred pounds. Photographs of him show an enormously fat man with a huge moon face. For a while he grew a beard and full curling moustache as if to conceal at least some of the weight.

Tough times were ahead for Texas, whose antipathy to government regulation had left the state open to all sorts of abuses by unrestrained capitalists. Hogg became aware of the tip of the iceberg when the Texas and Pacific Railway of millionaire "robber baron" Jay Gould stalled on extending its required line west from Longview to Dallas. Although the freight and passenger traffic would have made the line exceptionally profitable, the railroad wanted $100,000 in county bonds or they would change the route.

Hogg recognized that the officers of the company were playing Gregg County against Wood. So began his fight with the railroads, a fight that would ultimately drive Jay Gould out of Texas and create one of the first commissions to regulate businesses of all kinds. The fight would move him away from Wood County and the simple life forever. Ultimately, it would dominate his entire life.

Texas's fear and abhorrence of government regulation grew out of Reconstruction following the Civil War. At that time the state's almost totally Republican legislature included sixteen radicals who accepted bribes without qualm or conscience. Because of their control of both houses of the state legislature, Texas granted right-of-ways to allow two competing railroads to run parallel lines across the state on the condition that they would unite somewhere around El Paso.

Laying tracks across the lightly populated areas of West Texas as across the western United States was a costly process with little hope of commercial return. If private enterprise—namely the railroads—was to do this, they would require government subsidies. In fact, historians have shown that the total cost of laying track "from sea to shining sea" amounted to a tax of $28 on every American citizen from 1865 to 1873.

In Texas, reeling from the Civil War, the cost was heartbreaking. Under the behest of Republican Governor E. J. Davis, in 1870 the railroads were granted a $6 million subsidy, which forced Texas to issue thirty-year bonds paying eight percent, an extremely high rate in those days. Furthermore, the railroad gained title by right of eminent domain to 22 million acres of free Texas land. Under this ruinous contract, which incidentally practically guaranteed that no other Republican would be elected to office for the rest of the century, Texas's public debt doubled within six months.

The deal was such an obvious collusion between corruption and theft on such a shameful scale that everyone was angry and appalled. It could not be allowed to continue. Yet continue it did until 1874, ten years after the war when enough Texas citizens were able to vote to throw Davis out of office. Even then Davis refused to leave until an army of Texas irregulars massed in front of the capitol.

The call went out immediately thereafter to write a new state constitution. In an effort to be part of the writing of it, Hogg ran for the legislature. In his bid for election, he was defeated for the first and only time in his career.

Whether his presence in the legislature would have made any difference in the drafting of the post-reconstruction constitution is anybody's guess. After years of oppressive rule, the legislature was determined never to be subjugated again. Texas was left with a less than exemplary document that reflected the fears and prejudices of the Southern planters and ranchers, ex-Confederate soldiers, and the Democrats who wrote it.

Hogg's defeat whetted his appetite for battle. He ran and won the office of county attorney the next year and was sent as a delegate to the Democratic State Convention in Austin.

The problem of the railroads still had to be solved. Texas was by far the largest state in the Union with a largely agrarian population. It needed the rails to get its products to cities in a timely fashion. Instead of getting the excellent service such commerce deserved, the state was getting shoddy, outdated rolling stock operated at outrageous prices. For example, the dome of the new state capitol was put together in Belgium. It cost less to ship the monstrous pieces across the Atlantic than the railroad charged for the last two hundred miles to Austin.

New legislation was called for, but the Texas legislators failed to act to rein in these abuses largely because corporate pirates led by Jay Gould and his ilk were bribing them right and left. The new constitution paid the legislators only five dollars per day for the first sixty days and two dollars a day thereafter with a mileage allowance to and from Austin of five cents per mile. From this allowance they were supposed to pay for their food and lodging during the legislative session. The thinking was that only a professional man, well-to-do in his own right and dedicated to the common good, would take the office because he could not and would not take it to better himself financially. Unfortunately, the pittances left the legislators vulnerable to the powerful purses being waved underneath their noses.

Into this morass stepped James Stephen Hogg. At age thirty-five he ran for the office of attorney general. When he won, he found he couldn't afford to take the job since it paid only $2,000 a year. He took it anyway even though his family lived in straitened circumstances. That he was offered bribe after bribe is beyond question. Whether he accepted any of them is unknown. Very little scandal of any kind has ever attached itself to his name.

Instead, he became famous in the last days of the nineteenth century as an incorruptible force. His campaigns were run on the premise that "the people must rule the corporations or the corporations would rule and ruin the people."

In short order he attacked out-of-state insurance companies who were sending thousands of dollars annually back to Pennsylvania and New York and generally ignoring the laws to keep capital within the state. He caused to be passed laws forbidding foreign ownership of Texas land and severely restricted corporations' ownership of land not needed for the conduct of business.

He called to task the Capitol Syndicate of Chicago, the company formed to build the state capitol in Austin. When the capitol was finished, it leaked. He threatened them and the Capitol Freehold Land and Investment Company with confiscating the huge grant of land they had accepted as payment. The three million acres in the Panhandle was already on its way to becoming the famous XIT Ranch, the largest ranch in Texas. Convinced that the attorney general meant what he said, the syndicate fixed the leak.

Hogg's sights next turned on the Texas Traffic Association, a corporative alliance formed with Jay Gould's blessing, to agree to set rates for all railroads. Two railroads as well as five trunk lines now ran all the way across Texas: the Southern Pacific Railroad from Houston through San Antonio to El Paso and the Texas and Pacific from Texarkana through Dallas to El Paso. The stated purpose of the association was to reduce competitive pricing.

In reality, Texas Traffic was a monopoly to fix prices highly favorable to the railroads over the shippers and passengers. The so-called efficiency of the operation did not amount to lower freight rates for farmers, but more money in dividends and interest on inflated stocks and bonds for the stockholders of the railroads.

Moreover, Jay Gould had begun almost as soon as the tracks were laid to drain capital away from their maintenance and repairs as well as fail to replace rolling stock as it deteriorated.

Clearly a regulatory commission was necessary. Though Texans shuddered at the very mention of any kind of government regulation, Hogg, with his immense girth equaled only by his immense popularity, was able to ram it through. The job took him nearly four years. During that time he came to realize that the office of attorney general was not strong enough. He needed the bully pulpit of the governorship.

Unfortunately, his finances were in such a state that he really couldn't afford to run. The office paid $4,000 per annum, double the attorney general's office, but he couldn't afford to hold it. He was forced to borrow money left and right. Again, a lesser man would have succumbed to the temptations that were constantly offered to him, but no one ever knew James Stephen, as his sons called him, to accept a bribe.

When the Democratic Convention was held in San Antonio the summer of 1890, Jay Gould made a special trip to Texas to defeat him. During a speech in Dallas, he warned, "The attitude of the attorney general is such as to cause some fright among capitalists."

Hogg fought back with facts. In Georgia, Gould was allowed by law to haul lumber a hundred miles for only $14. The Texas and Pacific Line charged $80 to bring it the same distance out of the Piney Woods of East Texas to the center of commerce in Dallas. Trumpeting those and other statistics, Hogg "stumped" his way across Texas with great speeches directed to the soul of the dirt farmer who saw his profits going into the pockets of the railroads that shipped his produce.

Hogg was a great commoner, a "hoeman" champion. His speeches to the common people were as "folksy" as Lyndon Johnson's half a century later. He could speak for hours against railroads, insurance companies, industrialists, bloated capitalists, and gold. He would work up a sweat, throw off his coat, and roll up his sleeves, all the while making his great voice boom out of his huge chest. Then he'd shrug his suspenders off his shoulders, splash water on his face, and get his second wind. When he'd begin to speak again, the crowd would be hoarse with cheering.

At thirty-nine he won the nomination by a landslide. In a one-party state, it signified his election as governor in November.

Thoroughly alarmed, railroad lobbyists came out in force against him. Legislators were treated like princes to porterhouse steaks and rare wines, strong liquors, and weekend junkets to the Gulf Coast for gambling where they always won handsomely. Over and over the word was, "Don't be too hard on the railroads. Texas needs them. Hogg is a demagogue. He wants too much power."

In the end Hogg's commanding and demanding presence overcame the luxurious bribes. So was born the Texas Railroad Commission of 1890 patterned after the U.S. Interstate Commerce Act of 1887.

It exists to this day much as Hogg set it up. Three members are elected by statewide election in overlapping terms every two years. The chairmanship rotates among the members.

For the first chairman, Hogg wanted a man above reproach, a man no one could doubt would be unfailingly fair and honest. Such a man was John H. Reagan. He had served as the postmaster general of the Confederacy, had been imprisoned in a northern prison after the Civil War, had returned, reclaimed his citizenship at great personal cost, and now served Texas as her United States Senator. He was seventy years old and one of the most respected men in the state.

Summoning Reagan back from Washington, Hogg gave him a copy of the law that he had drafted and driven through the legislature with all the subtlety of a charging bull.

Reagan was amazed. "How was it that such a law as this got through?" he asked. "It is the best commission law I ever saw."

Hogg is said to have smiled almost winsomely. "It is the best law that has been passed in Texas in many a day and...I am going to reach up and get the curtains of heaven to clothe it in." He paused significantly. "Even if I have to pull somebody out of the United States Senate."

Reagan resigned before the end of his term.

In June 1891 the Texas Railroad Commission held its first meetings. Beginning as it meant to go on, it assumed the power to fix freight rates and passenger fares, which it immediately reduced. Even more important for later, it gained the power to control the issuance of railway stocks and bonds. No longer could such subsidies come from the legislature.

The railroads fought back in court, charging that the commission was wrong in principle, undemocratic, and unrepublican. When they lost, they mounted their campaign against Hogg, running George Clark, a conservative Democrat from Waco, who also happened to be a railway lawyer.

James Stephen Hogg

> **A VERY LITTLE GIANT ON A VERY RICKETY PLATFORM.**
>
> GOULD TOUCHES THE BUTTON, GEORGE TRIES HARD TO DO THE REST.

Cartoon from the *Texas Farmer*, October 22, 1892, portrays Governor Hogg as Jack the Giant-Killer. Jay Gould, the railroad tycoon, pushes the buttons from Washington, D.C.

Hogg, the supreme campaigner, met Clark, a former Confederate from Alabama, before 8,000 people at the town of Cameron about halfway between Austin and Waco. Clark had vowed to "Turn Texas Loose" from Hogg's demagoguery.

Many people had come from both towns by special train. They were unruly and noisy. The candidates could not make themselves heard, but Hogg won the hearts and minds of the crowd by doing something that Texans talked about for years.

Texas Politicians: Good 'n' Bad

> **HOW WE ARE RIDDEN.**
>
> A sell-out press rides the people.
> Clark rides a sell-out press and the people.
> The whole business is straddled by Gould and "alch."

Cartoon from the *Texas Farmer*, May 7, 1892, shows the strength of big business. Belo Publishing (present-day owner of *The Dallas Morning News* as well as a chain of television stations across the nation) is portrayed as trampling the people of Texas while carrying both Gould and Clark.

Pausing in his speech, Clark, breathless and hoarse, poured himself a glass of water. As he set the empty glass down, Hogg rose, picked up the pitcher, and drank the rest of the water down without taking a breath. The crowd erupted into cheers, thrilled at the sight of the big man they claimed as their own, slaking his thirst in a matter-of-fact, rude manner.

At the Democratic Convention in Houston, two delegations appeared—one to nominate Hogg, one to nominate Clark. Neither side was willing to compromise. Two temporary chairmen were lifted onto a stage. The work of two separate conventions began side by side. Each chairman made welcoming speeches and got on with recognizing the delegates and preparing a platform.

Inside the auditorium was bedlam.

Out in the hall, close to fifty fistfights broke out.

Ima Hogg with the official portrait of her father Governor James Stephen Hogg.
Center for American History, UT-Austin

In the end Hogg won the election going away, and the Railroad Commission remains in power to this day. Decades later it became the state's regulatory agency for the oil industry as well. Its importance there far overshadowed its original significance. It is responsible for regulating much that is good in Texas.

Though many of its official duties now are the responsibility of the Texas Department of Transportation, it generally acts as a watchdog organization, correcting the abuses of power within the state. It still has intrastate authority over railroad safety, truck lines, buses, and the pipelines by which the oil and gas industry moves its products.

From Spindletop to Swindletop

When James Hogg left office in 1895, he had $136 dollars in the bank and was thousands of dollars in debt. He had been an honest man to the detriment of his family and his own prospects of security in his old age. Still, he was only forty-four years old. He had plenty of time to make his fortune. With the self-assurance that he had been born with, he could set up a lucrative law practice.

As he set about making his living in Houston, exciting things were happening just a few miles away, things totally unexpected, things that would make fortunes.

The North boasted that nothing worth mining was to be found south of the Mason-Dixon Line. In this they were proved incontrovertibly wrong.

The little town of Corsicana, just fifty miles south of Dallas, was drilling for a reliable water supply. A special company had been hired to put down three artesian wells within the city limits. Using an old-fashioned cable tool rig and a wooden derrick, the company ran a drill down 1,035 feet. Ugly, malodorous oil bubbled out of the hole.

What a nuisance!

The company diverted it into a ditch, sank a metal casing to seal the stuff off, and continued the search for water. Still the oil continued to rise.

The company refused to be discouraged. They continued to drain the black gunk off into a ditch at the rate of about 150 gallons a day. Despite this irksome problem, they drilled until finally at the depth of 2,470 feet, they struck water that supplied Corsicana for many years. The drillers took their money and went home.

Then two profit-minded men sent a sample of the runoff to a laboratory operated by Standard Oil in Pennsylvania. They learned that the oil was of commercial quality. That is to say that it was suitable for burning in lamps. In 1895 it must be remembered that there were only five automobiles in the entire United States.

For another couple of years, nothing much happened until "Buckskin Joe" Cullinan, a Standard Oil executive, came through. He claimed that he was an independent oilman. However, after he looked around, he formed a company backed by officials from the Rockefeller organization. "Buckskin Joe" found he could bring in very shallow wells at depths ranging from 1,000 to 2,000 feet. The expense was low. The profit was high. Soon he found the money to build his own refinery, the first west of the Mississippi. He gave Texas its very first oil boomtown. In 1898 the Corsicana field produced more than a half million barrels of oil.

Texas needed James Stephen Hogg to bust the trusts that came flocking in, but by that time he was long gone, seeking his own fortune. Fortunately, his laws against developers taking money out of the state, originally invoked against insurance companies, helped to an extent.

Texas Politicians: Good 'n' Bad

Captain Anthony Lucas, the owner of Spindletop, found his way from the Polytechnic Institute at Graz, Austria, to the discovery that dramatically changed the world forever.
American Petroleum Institute

Meanwhile a truly independent oilman, Patillo Higgins, was looking at thirty-three acres on a slope called Big Hill near Beaumont, then a sleepy farm hamlet in the center of rice paddies. Farmers in and around the town actually had used Big Hill. It was a wallow where they brought their hogs to let the sulfur water kill their fleas and cure their mange.

Undaunted by the smell or the unpromising reputation, Higgins tapped all his friends for money. He contacted Standard Oil, who sent a representative who was unimpressed. When all else failed, he advertised. In 1899 Anthony F. Lucas of Louisiana answered his ad. Higgins took him to the long-neglected hill.

Captain Lucas was an adventurer and above all a gambler. The general lore is that no one can be an oilman who is not a gambler. The Austrian mining engineer had graduated from the Polytechnic Institute in Graz. Although he was looking for sulfur, upon inspecting the sight, he decided he would settle for oil. He was fairly certain that he was looking at the top of an underground salt dome pushed upward by pressure from below. Oil was often found around them.

In June 1899 he signed a lease for 663 acres with an option to buy. He made a down payment of $11,150 cash with some $20,000 still owed. Patillo Higgins was to have ten percent interest in whatever was found.

Lucas began drilling almost immediately. His first well went down to 575 feet before his light piping collapsed. However, the bit was bringing up oil before he was forced to stop.

Underfinanced, he sought backers for more than a year without much success. Against his better judgment he too tried Standard Oil, whose geologist again deemed Big Hill "unpromising." James Hogg's stringent laws that forbade corporations from taking money earned in Texas out of the state undoubtedly played a part in deterring the Rockefellers from advancing any money. In the end Lucas was able to get $300,000 from Andrew

W. Mellon, who was on his way to becoming America's fourth billionaire.

Lucas then went to Corsicana. He reasoned that the mild "boomtown" must contain a number of men who believed in Texas oil. There he arranged to meet the man whom knowledgeable oilmen considered the most capable drilling contractor in the country. His name was Jim Hamill.

Lucas must have done some powerful persuading. The Hamill brothers—Jim, Curt, and Al—agreed to come and work for Lucas at $55 a month plus expenses of $2.00 a foot for three wells. In early October 1900 the Hamills arrived in Beaumont.

They built a wooden derrick out of wet, green timber and began "spudding in" the well—boring in with a twelve-inch drill bit on a rotary rig. Unlike the cable tool, which was like driving in a nail, the rotary rig was like putting in a screw. The "fishtail" bit attached to the pipe was rotated from the surface. When water was pumped down the hole to keep the bit cool, it flushed the cuttings up the outside of the pipe. It was ideal for the Texas Gulf Coast where soft formations such as quicksands made drilling a nightmare. Water was later replaced by mud to make the hole even more stable.

Despite some early success, more problems ensued until Hamill's helpers were quitting in disgust, and the brothers themselves were in despair as to how to get the job done. Despite inventing new techniques almost daily and discovering new ways to drill, they were only three hundred feet farther than Captain Lucas had been on the day his piping had collapsed.

Then on a cold midnight in December, the drilling suddenly became easier. The bit began to spin. Al Hamill detected oil in the slush pit. By breakfast time they were getting a big showing of oil.

Captain Lucas excitedly asked how much it would bring in. Al Hamill hazarded what was a daring figure for the time, "I think it will easily bring in fifty barrels a day."

Such an amount was almost unheard of. At that point they almost stopped drilling and started pumping, but one of their backers suggested that they go another three hundred feet—just to see what might be underneath.

On New Year's Day, 1901, they drilled another 150 feet. At 1,020 feet the bit gave out. Al Hamill wired Corsicana for a new one. On January 10 it came in on the freight train. Hamill brought it back to the well in his buggy. With the new bit on, they lowered 700 feet of drill pipe down the hole.

Suddenly, the hole began to spout mud.

Curt Hamill was perched high on the derrick on the monkey board, directing the operation. Muck shot up into his face. It filled his eyes and his nose. Pelted by it, heavy pipes shooting by his head like cannon shells through the top of the derrick, he managed to scramble down. All three brothers and helper Peck Byrd fled in terror as the pipes came crashing down all around them. At last, all was quiet.

Miraculously no one had been hurt.

But the well was a mess of ruined equipment and slippery, gooey mud.

When they could wipe their faces and hands enough to get to work, they began to shovel the mud off the derrick floor, muttering and groaning at the wreck and their bad luck.

Suddenly, from beneath their feet came a deafening roar, and the well erupted like a volcano. More mud, then gas, oil, and rock shot hundreds of feet into the air.

Aghast, they staggered back as they witnessed what no man on earth had ever witnessed before—a gusher—a wild well blowing in.

In the midst of it all, Curt Hamill remembered the boiler. "We've got to get that fire out!" he yelled.

Texas Politicians: Good 'n' Bad

The Lucas Gusher at Spindletop, January 10, 1901. People could see it for miles around. The lake of oil it formed contained at least a million barrels.
Texas Mid-Continent Oil & Gas Association

Oil showered all around them as they threw buckets of water on the firebox until the last spark was doused.

Peck Byrd ran for Captain Lucas, who came up over the hill whipping his horse into a full run. From the distance he could see what was happening, but he could not believe his eyes. He jumped from the buggy and ran to the brothers who were by this time dancing around and congratulating themselves.

"Al! Al!" he shouted. "What is it?"

"Oil, Captain—it's oil!"

"Thank God!" Lucas cried.

Like Old Faithful geyser, the oil could be seen for miles. Crowds of farmers and ranchers and their wives came to see the phenomenon. A rancher rode into Beaumont shouting, "They've got a wild oil well out at the hill and the damn thing's ruinin' my land!"

Within an hour Beaumont too emptied out. Everyone came to stand in awe of the black giant and the lake of oil that was forming ever wider around its feet. Watchmen had to be hired on the spot to prevent people from smoking.

Ironically, Patillo Higgins was the last one in town to know. He had been out trying to put together a lumber deal to clear away his debt. When he came back in, newspaper reporters interviewed him. All he could remember or really knew at that time was the name the real estate company had given his thirty-three acres on the hill.

The company had called it Spindletop Heights.

Texas Politicians: Good 'n' Bad

The Rush for Black Gold

What happened next made the California Gold Rush of the nineteenth century seem like a gentle rain. A tornado struck Texas in the form of literally thousands of men coming for oil.

The story was told that a reporter from St. Louis stepped off the train in Beaumont. He was immediately offered a lease for $1,000. He refused, but the man behind him bought it, then sold it to someone else for $5,000, only to see it sold almost immediately for $20,000.

A real estate promoter named D. R. Beatty arrived the day after the gusher blew in, leased ten acres in Spindletop Heights, and began drilling. A Klondike gold rusher grabbed the first train from San Francisco, leased fifteen acres from Higgins, and had a well going down. The Hamill brothers began drilling two more wells near their first.

There was so much oil. Nobody seemed to mind who owned it.

During the Beaumont boom, an acre of land at Spindletop itself sold for $1,000,000 and none less than $200,000.

For nine days the well spouted oil. Finally, the Hamill brothers managed to get it capped. A million barrels of oil formed a shallow lake around the sand mound where the well had been drilled. It was a depressing sight, and the bankers were not really sure what it meant. Was that all there was?

Then on March 3 a spark from a train set the million-barrel lake afire. Before the fire was out, Beatty's well roared in. Other wells followed as the world could not believe that six oil wells were spouting at once in Beaumont, Texas, at the hill called Spindletop. Moreover, the six wells produced in one day as much as all the oil wells in the entire world.

Beaumont, even Texas herself, was unprepared for what happened after that. Such waste, such profligacy. Men were

James Stephen Hogg

dissatisfied with a well that didn't gush. They thought the exciting sight was part of the process.

Of course, many hundreds came with money in their pockets and went away empty-handed. Graft and swindling seemed to be part and parcel of the game—just as claim jumping had been in California.

"Buckskin Joe" Cullinan came from Corsicana, took one look at what was happening, and organized the Texas Fuel Company for purchasing oil and operating a pipeline. No fool he, Cullinan recognized that money was to be made transporting the oil that was spouting toward the skies. At that point no one had even thought about that or any other aspect of the business.

One who came to seek his fortune was James Hogg.

Remembered by everyone who ever saw him, respected throughout the state, the Houston lawyer formed a partnership with James Swayne of Fort Worth, who had been the floor leader of the Texas House during Hogg's terms as governor. Taking in five other men, they managed to scrape together $40,000 to form the Hogg-Swayne Syndicate. It was never incorporated because Hogg was dead set against anything that smacked of corporations.

Certainly, James Hogg needed and wanted to make some serious money. Perhaps also in the back of his mind, by joining with his old friend, a man whom he considered to be as honest as he was, he hoped to set the tone for this new and exciting industry that was gushing forth in Beaumont.

Hogg tried first to negotiate with Lucas, but everything the captain owned or leased was already tied up by his partners Guffey Petroleum Company. In the end Hogg had to go to James Guffey, who negotiated as shrewdly with the former governor as he had with the Austrian mining engineer. For $310,000 Hogg was able to get both surface and mineral rights to fifteen acres.

It was a sweet deal for Hogg because in a very short time it was worth twice that, but the sweetest deal was for Guffey. He had snared the most respected man in Texas as one of his conglomerate. Guffey was a Yankee, not a popular thing to be around Beaumont, only a few miles from Sabine Pass where Dick Dowling had met the invading force and thrown them back into the sea. He was also fairly certain that he needed strong Texas friendships in the event that Standard Oil tried to move in on Spindletop.

Hogg was his shield and buckler.

Meanwhile, Hogg was in trouble. Where was the $310,000 coming from in a syndicate that had only $40,000 in capital?

Hogg suggested selling small leases on the Hogg-Swayne track. While his defensive maneuvers were perfectly legal, they spelled the beginning of the end for Spindletop.

While the Syndicate retained for itself half the fifteen acres the owners had purchased, it leased small blocks of land, some as small as a thirty-second of an acre. The land became so subdivided that as the wells went in seeking to capture the wild oil, the legs of the derricks interlaced. A man could walk the floors of one derrick after another to the end of the street without touching the ground.

Some of the subdivisions were subdivided further. Leases grew so small that the wells no longer had room for the boilers. Those necessary pieces of equipment had to be placed out in the road, which became known as Boiler Avenue.

The law of capture, by which oil was governed, came into play with tragic results. The price of oil fell to three cents a barrel while drinking water sold for a nickel a cup. Men drilled and drilled. The associated gas pressure, which had created the exciting gushers, decreased. The necessity for it was not understood. Conservation was an unknown word.

James Stephen Hogg

Throughout 1901 the drilling went on unabated. Every person who could concentrated on pumping all he could out of the earth as fast as he could.

James Hogg took the train from Houston at least once a month. While he was in town, he visited Spindletop several times a week. Able to pay off some of his debts now, he was much happier even wading through the weeds to get to his wells. There he shook hands with all the roughnecks and talked in his folksy way as if he were one of them. Weighing close to three hundred pounds and sweating profusely in the terrible heat and humidity, he would tromp back into Beaumont, where he'd pay two bootblacks to work on his big boots at the Pearl Street café. It gave him great pleasure to think that he had never really abandoned the simple country life.

In March he provided for his family by obtaining a contract to buy 4,100 acres of land in Brazoria County. The price was $30,000 or approximately seven dollars per acre. After buying the land, which he named Varner Plantation after one of the later Texas impresarios, he learned that a lighted match would start fires from gas fumes escaping from the earth where artesian water bubbled up. He was excited at the prospect of owning his own oil field, but by the time he had clear title to the land, he could find no one to drill. The price of oil had fallen too low.

He never stopped thinking and planning for the people. One day he remarked that the legislature ought to pass a law that the people of Texas would never have to pay over twenty cents a barrel for oil produced in the state.

Likewise, he never understood the damage Hogg-Swayne had done by leasing such tiny parcels of land. In fact, his syndicate knew next to nothing about business. They were a group of politicians and lawyers. They needed a man who knew and understood the oil business.

They needed "Buckskin Joe" Cullinan, who organized the Texas Fuel Company. He had built a 37,000-barrel storage tank twenty miles from the field. He bought cheap oil and stored it to wait for prices to climb. He had also purchased the right-of-way for a pipeline to Port Arthur.

To capitalize it, he sold $50,000 worth of stock to Hogg-Swayne—$50,000 which they did not then have in hand. There was no money to be had in Texas. Everyone was stretched to the limit as they sought to invest in their dreams.

So Hogg, the great persuader, accompanied by his pretty nineteen-year-old daughter, headed east to find investors. His target was a traveling salesman for barbed wire—"Bet-a-Million" Gates. One of the most daring men in New York, Gates bet $10,000 on the toss of a coin. He and others had founded the American Steel and Wire Company, worth $90 million. He took pride in the fact that the Four Hundred never accepted him socially. Part of his legend was that he laughed at society and cultivated gross behavior and bad manners. He practiced being rude, crude, and generally obnoxious.

James Hogg's daughter Ima, who was named for the heroine of his uncle Thomas's romantic book *The Fate of Marvin,* a novel long out of print, remembered Gates as a man who went out of his way to shock. Although he had an amazing amount of knowledge on the tip of his tongue, he never allowed himself a moment to relax and be himself.

Hogg got the money. Ironically, he helped form a corporation whose board included five men from the North and four men from Texas. As a lawyer, Hogg failed utterly to get in writing the stipulations he prized: that the headquarters of the Texas Company would never leave Texas and that a majority of the board must be Texans. Whether he believed that a handshake and a verbal agreement were all that were necessary, no one will ever know.

When the nine-member-board was formed, Cullinan from Pennsylvania actually lived in Texas. Therefore, he was deemed the fifth Texan.

Likewise, no one will ever know what pressures were brought to bear on Hogg from all sides. Certainly, the fiery governor of the last century would never have agreed to such a thing. As the company began to operate, he became alarmed. The Texas Company began to "smell like Standard Oil," he told his friends. "I'm going to get out of it at the first opportunity."

By August 30, 1901, forty gushers were flowing from Spindletop. Sixty individuals, fifty oil companies, and two supply concerns adopted rules for the use of the field, in particular to avoid the disastrous fires that now began to plague the area where no one could put down a foot without sinking in oily muck. They created eleven regulations which all agreed to abide by. Primarily they concerned carrying matches, smoking, and carrying lanterns, but one forbade the opening of wellheads to let gushers shoot a hundred feet in the air for the entertainment of passengers on the trains.

By the end of 1901, Spindletop had produced 4,393,000 barrels of oil—*with no new developments for its uses or for potential by-products.*

In 1902 James Hogg was in trouble again financially. He became director of a Beaumont bank, which quickly developed irregularities. He and his family were beside themselves with disgust and embarrassment.

Someone asked Hogg if the Texas Railroad Commission had the authority to take an interest in providing cars to handle the oil traffic, which now seemed headed for Port Arthur where tankers were arriving daily to take on loads bound for eastern markets.

Hogg was delighted to remember the details of the commission he had worked so hard to effect. It did! His commission could handle this and so much more. If he were governor, he would see to it. But he wasn't governor. Governor Samuel Lanham was more interested in creating new colleges and shoring up existing universities for Texas's growing population.

Hogg sailed for England to try to tap British investment capital. Going hat in hand must have galled him. He had always maintained Texas was for Texans. At least in London he enjoyed social success. The ambassador arranged for him to receive an invitation for an official presentation to the King. Hogg declined because of the incongruous figure he would cut in the required knee breeches, silk stockings, and cutaway coat.

Even though he was embarrassed and disappointed, he learned that the British were swiftly converting their locomotives to fuel oil. "Even paying high transportation charges from Beaumont to London," he wrote, "they find oil much cheaper and more satisfactory for steam purposes than coal."

He returned to Texas with no money, but sure that new markets were going to open. He continued to work to buy land around the state that looked promising for oil. He signed on with various law firms then resigned his position as he discovered that they wanted his name, but not his opinions.

His fortunes continued to slip. His wife was dead. His sons were earning their own ways, but his daughter needed a secure future. What was he going to do?

"The Standard Oil Senator"

Joseph Weldon Bailey

"No honest man can misunderstand the transaction and no scoundrel can ever again successfully misrepresent me."

Big Oil Comes to the Party

While the production of the Corsicana field might have seemed too little to matter to the eastern oil corporations, events in 1901 convinced them that they needed to be in Texas. While it was a "wretched" place, undereducated and uncivilized, the unparalleled eruption of liquid wealth that was Spindletop convinced many that it was the place to be. Millions of barrels of oil, each barrel equaling forty-two gallons of light sweet crude, was more than Pennsylvania, Ohio, and the rest of the world combined had ever produced.

Without a doubt the phenomenon of Spindletop led to the conversion of railroads from coal to oil. The locomotive's great black trail that covered the passengers in cinders and ash became a thing of the past. No longer would ladies have to keep their veils down over their faces and cover their clothing with dusters to keep them from being burned.

At the beginning of the twentieth century, three types of engines—steam, electric, and gasoline—were competing to be the one that would propel the newly invented automobile.

Although almost everyone still used horses as beasts for transportation, inventors touted the car as the clean, pollution-free alternative to the piles of dung in the city streets left by the animals. With the sudden appearance of exceedingly cheap oil, steam and electric engines disappeared, and the internal combustion engine with its attendant smog has been with us for a century.

When Spindletop blew in, how John D. Rockefeller must have snarled at the geologists who had seen no promise in the Texas field! How they must have felt as they crept out of his office in disgrace! For the first time in its history, Standard Oil was late to the party. Not just late but on the outside looking in.

Immediately, it took steps to catch up. The company set a priority to acquire key pieces of property within the state, which, thanks to Hogg, had a firm anti-big-business attitude.

Of course Rockefeller had heard of the experiences of the insurance companies and the railroads. Jay Gould and he were part of the fabulous Four Hundred. They knew each other and dealt with many of the same people. Jay Gould had undoubtedly cursed Attorney General and then Governor James Hogg and his laws unfavorable to out-of-state ownership and, above all, his regulatory Texas Railroad Commission.

The trick for Rockefeller was to get in before any more damage—that is, any restraint of unbridled capitalism—was done. The obvious candidate for a bribe would have been James Hogg himself. By his own declaration, Hogg was broke. As a representative of the newly formed Hogg-Swayne Syndicate, he came East with hat in hand. The offer of enough to pay all of his debts and put him on a legal retainer for life was on the table—if he would accept the strings attached to it.

To Rockefeller's chagrin and frustration, Hogg would not be bribed. He would not take the money offered him in exchange for one iota of control in his beloved state.

Fortunately for Rockefeller, there were other men, men who wouldn't refuse the opportunity to get rich, particularly if they could be convinced that what they were doing was really for the good of their constituency—in the long run.

Joseph Weldon Bailey seemed from his youth the man to fill the bill. Born in Crystal Springs, Mississippi, he attended five different colleges and universities before completing his law degree in 1883. Immediately thereafter, he plunged into local Mississippi politics where he defeated his own father for delegate to the state Democratic Convention. The issue was railroad regulation, which young Bailey said he favored.

In the next year, however, he was accused of illegal activities. Before the election, he had threatened and intimidated black voters. Since half the county was black, the black voters refused to go away quietly. Complaints were brought in New Orleans before a United State Senate Committee investigating the incident. In the end no action was taken against Bailey on the provision that he act with dispatch. The suggested action was that he leave the state rather than perjure himself.

"Good riddance to bad rubbish," seemed the general consensus of opinion.

Unchastened, Joe Bailey moved to North Texas where in 1890 he was elected to the U.S. House of Representatives from his home in Gainesville. At twenty-seven, he was the youngest member in the House. In Washington he voted the party line, and back in Austin he spent much of his time kowtowing to Jim Hogg during his terms as attorney general and then as governor.

According to Ima Hogg, her father never trusted him. Bailey would always sidle over and whisper rather than ally himself openly with the governor. Bailey played politics for all he was worth rather than take a stand that would alienate a single voter.

Joseph W. Bailey.
Texas politics sank to a new low with him.
Center for American Studies, UT-Austin

Then in 1900 Bailey and Hogg seemed destined for a collision course. Bailey entered the race for U.S. Senate, setting a campaign pace from east to west across Texas, visiting as many state legislators as he could. He did not speak to people across the state as might have been expected of a candidate to represent them in the highest legislative body in the land.

The original Constitution provided that the senators of the United States should be chosen by the *legislature* of each state for a term of six years. The provision was another safeguard inserted by the document's framers, who did not trust the "uneducated" majority to choose their long-term legislators wisely. The idea was that the people would exert their will through their elected representatives whose comparatively short two-year terms would allow the voters to correct any mistakes they might have made.

Bailey had chosen to campaign as a result of rumors bruited about in the U.S. Senate. By April 1900 the senatorial incumbent, elderly Horace Chilton, was so ill that he withdrew from the race. Unopposed, Bailey would be one of two U.S. senators at the very youthful age of thirty-seven. The only fly in his ointment was that many Texas politicians thought that James Hogg would be the ideal person to replace Chilton to represent Texas.

Bailey saw Hogg as his enemy whom he must discredit in order to defeat. He couldn't believe that Hogg would turn down the office if it were offered to him. A supremely ambitious man, Bailey was sure that a powerful politician with the kind of support that Hogg's very name could generate would leap at the chance to become senator.

While Hogg was going about the state making speeches for the presidency of Democrat William Jennings Bryan, Bailey was in Austin ostensibly to "plan strategy for the Democratic Convention" but in reality to garner serious, powerful support for his candidacy.

The man willing to provide the support was Henry Clay Pierce, president of the Waters-Pierce Oil Company, who was determined to continue to do business in Texas. In 1894 Waters-Pierce had been found to be a subsidiary of Standard Oil, which was held at that time to be a monopoly and "a conspiracy against trade." The companies had been the targets of an investigation and prosecution by then attorney general of Texas Martin M. Crane. Arguing for the people, Crane declared, "... ninety-nine percent of the oil business of Texas amounting to one-half million barrels annually" had been controlled by Waters-Pierce in trust for Standard Oil.

A Texas lobbyist. With legislators' stipends so low, many fell easy prey to a few extra dollars.

Joseph Weldon Bailey

Crane further accused Waters-Pierce of seeking to eliminate competition by rebating customers for refusing to handle any other company's oil. This rebate came in addition to underselling rivals for the express purpose of putting them out of business. When Waters-Pierce—subsidized by Standard Oil—became the only source of oil, they then would—as they had done in other states—raise prices unreasonably. Crane further discovered that eventually all stock in the company was transferred into the Standard Oil trust.

The suit had rocked on for three years, as suits of this nature will, through delays and appeals. Lawyers and lobbyists were thick in the halls of justice and in the capitol in Austin.

Waters-Pierce had a fortune at stake in Texas. The firm had three hundred distribution stations—investments worth half a million dollars. They were determined not to allow themselves to be forced out. Although oil as fuel for transportation was in its infancy, illuminating oils were running neck and neck with gas, which had proved dangerous to consumers in its natural colorless and odorless state. Electricity was largely unknown.

Joseph Bailey appeared at the right time to "assist" Pierce in winding up the suit. The unscrupulous young man was at that time in need of money. He had gone into debt purchasing land and blooded horses in Kentucky and Texas, where he had worked a deal to obtain the Gibbs ranch near Dallas in exchange for a much larger one in West Texas. Bailey had to come up with $4,000 cash to complete the exchange. He also needed to raise even more to bring his new Kentucky holding into working order.

Former Governor David R. Francis, a friend of Bailey's from St. Louis, Missouri, where Waters-Pierce was based, approached him. Francis told the "wanna-be" senator that Standard Oil was really a good company, a fine business, that was being "pushed around" by people like Hogg, who was probably jealous of other people's cleverness and good fortune.

Texas Politicians: Good 'n' Bad

Everyone knew that Hogg didn't have a head for business. One only had to look at the mess he'd made of his own finances.

On the other hand Bailey could help Texans, perhaps even save them from themselves, if he would just represent Waters-Pierce before the Court of Appeals. Just by adding his name to their team of lawyers, he would sway the judges.

Of course he'd be paid handsomely. Did he need four thousand dollars for his ranch near Dallas? He'd earn it. Did his stock farm in Kentucky need upgrading and restoring? Five thousand dollars' worth of repairs were no problem. This case was going to require many hours of research. But, of course, the law clerks could do most of it.

As a matter of fact the sums that Bailey borrowed—over ten thousand dollars—were entered into the company books under the account of "Texas legal expenses." Had Pierce not assumed part of them as a personal loan, the courts could never have proved any collusion or bribery.

In 1897 a Texas jury had rendered a verdict against Waters-Pierce, canceling their charter to do business in Texas. Pierce himself was placed under indictment at that time. But more appeals went on for three more years. At last in 1900, despite having Bailey on his "dream team," the United States Supreme Court sustained the lower court's rulings.

Determined to earn his money or perhaps determined not to be found out, Bailey then went to the man who would be Texas's new attorney general, Thomas Smith, and supposedly "promised that Waters-Pierce would be good."

By that time Smith was on to Bailey, as was almost everyone in any position higher than errand boy. Smith pointed out that "promising to be good" wasn't enough. He suggested that the company go back to Missouri, dissolve all their ties to Standard Oil, and then return with clean hands to take an oath to obey the Texas laws. At that time, Smith promised he would do all he could to aid them to obtain a new charter to operate in Texas.

Of course Pierce had no intention of dissolving anything with Standard Oil. In fact, he couldn't have dissolved anything. He was the front man for Rockefeller. Pierce went to Waco to talk with George Clark, Hogg's old political rival of the "screaming match" at the 1896 Democratic Convention. Clark pulled in all the political favors at his disposal to get the cash settlement reduced in the civil suit and to get McLennan County Attorney Cullen Thomas to drop the criminal indictment.

While Thomas seemed to be having trouble making up his mind, Clark offered to "split" Pierce's generous fee. The offer to split a fee with the defendant's attorney was tantamount to offer of a bribe.

To his credit Thomas refused.

At this point Pierce called on Joe Bailey to earn his money. Or perhaps the young man was simply eager to prove that he was actually worth the personal loan that now came to $13,300. Bailey went immediately to St. Louis where he obtained a new charter, declaring the old Waters-Pierce Oil Company dissolved. Bailey returned to Austin with the reorganized charter in his hands. Holding a news conference, he announced proudly that he had been responsible for bringing a new company into Texas—one that would be fair to everyone. When asked, he declared that Waters-Pierce had absolutely no control from Standard Oil. Waters-Pierce, he maintained, "always complied with the laws of every state."

Of course, by that time, few people believed him. Public reaction to the reappearance of Waters-Pierce was unfavorable. What followed was a fight that Joe Bailey could not afford to lose. Senator was the big leap forward for his career. He had to be elected by the Democratic Party Convention in August. The legislature would rubber-stamp it, and he would be off to Washington, D.C.

The Texans who cared knew a wolf, no matter how much lamb's wool it shed. Horace Chilton's supporters decided to draft Governor Hogg to pick up the standard the old senator had laid down.

"Your friends will elect you United States senator if you will allow them," Waller Baker of Waco telegraphed Hogg.

"It will take a lifetime as a private citizen for me to pay my debts," Hogg replied regretfully. "I cannot incur further liabilities."

Too Hot to Handle

Once back in Texas, Pierce spread his largesse far and wide. Lobbyists entertained the delegates to the convention in Austin and then the state and national congressmen and senators royally, always with the same litany—*big oil isn't really so bad. We need the revenue it can bring to the state. Beyond wells they'll build refineries and pipelines. They know how to get the job done.*

Bailey's star shone ever brighter. He was determined to be approved for Chilton's Senate seat. Waters-Pierce too made their presence known. They were supremely confident of their welcome by virtue of the money they had to spread around. If the cost of doing business as usual included "buying" a convention, the company was prepared to do that too. It was a small price to pay for half a million a year in revenue.

Meanwhile the stories were circulating about the Gibbs ranch "deal." When the Democrats assembled for their convention on June 20, Bailey must have been aware of the rumors. Still, he believed that he had a clear majority with no significant candidate, such as James Stephen Hogg, to run against him.

Let Hogg come from the Governor's Mansion if he dared! On the other hand, if Hogg, the sitting governor of Texas albeit a lame duck, stepped onto the floor of the Democratic Convention, Bailey had to be prepared to fight. He and his boss Waters-Pierce differed greatly from Hogg on significant points that the delegates should support on the Democratic platform. To that end the delegates were provided with food and plenty to drink by the corporation in the name of Joe Bailey.

The mood of good feeling and camaraderie spread over the convention floor. Though rumors circulated of illegal tactics and "deals," Bailey was in control thanks to Pierce's intense lobbying. The one possible hitch in his senatorial ambitions was a senatorial speech by Hogg, whose power to sway men to his thinking was legend. Bailey was truly afraid of him.

The hopeful candidate's strategy was to strike first. When Hogg arrived, Bailey would have already won the convention to his side. He made a dramatic speech, pretending to quote a conversation between himself and Pierce in which he told Pierce sternly what the businessman must do. Bailey presented himself as saying, "I do not believe the people of Texas will tolerate the methods of the Standard Oil Company."

According to Bailey, Pierce replied, "We are not a part of the Standard Oil Company. The Standard Oil Company has never owned a controlling interest in our company."

Bailey then challenged him to come to the Texas convention and tell the Democratic officers that Waters-Pierce would abide by their laws. He also recounted his adamant refusal to work for Pierce. "No, Sir; you haven't got money enough to hire me."

At this point the Bailey delegates broke into cheers. Some members of the delegation tried to question Bailey. One in particular pointed out—when he could make himself heard—that Pierce was a criminal under indictment in the state of Texas while Bailey was negotiating with him.

The rabble-rousers drowned the dissenting voice out. For Bailey everything looked good. He and his bullyboys had shouted down the opposition. Washington was in his sights.

To his consternation James Hogg did come. The man from Cherokee County had never run from a fight in his life. At the insistence of friends and supporters, he came onto the floor to present the minority report. To his disgust and to the anger of his supporters, he learned that the hall was Bailey's territory. The man who was the sitting governor of Texas was booed in his own state.

As the chairman tried to get the convention under control, Hogg stared at the men in the front rows, who were openly jeering and catcalling. Suddenly, he recognized the reason for their behavior.

"Gentlemen," he shouted suddenly. "I know you are drunk."

The jeers grew louder accompanied by howls and hisses.

Gaveling for order did no good. But Hogg would not yield the floor. Above their noise he boomed, "The material question presented by the re-permission of the Waters-Pierce Oil Company to do business in this state is: Shall Texas or the trusts control?"

How Bailey must have cringed inwardly! Any minute he expected that Hogg would burst into a denunciation of his "deals" and illegal tactics. He never once doubted that Hogg had come onto the floor for the express purpose of accepting the Senate seat when it was offered to him. He was equally fearful that he could not defeat a man with Hogg's reputation.

Angry and a little bit afraid, Bailey sprang to his feet and delivered a ringing speech against the influence of the former governor whom he characterized as a demagogue whose day was over. Bailey thundered, "If there were an anti-Bailey party, I call upon all right-thinking delegates to crush it out."

But Hogg did not criticize Bailey or dispute his right to have the Senate seat. Since he had no intention of taking it himself, he left that to others. Instead, he called upon the delegates to defeat the Republicans, whose gods were business and money to the detriment of the common man.

Former Attorney General Martin Crane spoke after Hogg, pointing out that Waters-Pierce had never stopped operating for the three years since the indictment was handed down against them, nor had they paid the fines assessed to them.

A Dallas *News* reporter called it the "most acrimonious and bitter fight in the history of the Democratic Party."

In the late evening Hogg spoke again to present three proposals to be included in the platform. A near-riot ensued. Hogg was allowed to speak only after the Travis County sheriff and the sergeants-at-arms belabored the delegates for five minutes to get some degree of order.

His speech this time consisted of simple recommendations with regard to the Texas Railroad Commission, which had been Hogg's baby from its inception. Though they represented regulation of the railroads, Clay Pierce saw them as setting a precedent that would ultimately damage the fledgling oil industry.

He was right, as events would later prove, and at that time he instructed Bailey to keep the proposals from coming to the floor if possible. If they did manage to come before the delegates in the form of a motion, Bailey's constituents were to vote the recommendations down at all costs.

In the end Hogg's great oratory was able to sway the convention to include the Railroad Commission's recommendations in the platform, but it was a pyrrhic victory for him. Others spoke against him, further undermining his legacy.

Bailey and too many of the other delegates nodded their heads in approval but did not vote as Hogg demanded. Their gods were already money and business. Although everyone knew that Bailey campaigned across Texas financed by oil trust men with rumors of illegal land deals clinging to his coattails, not enough people cared to do anything about him.

When the legislature convened in Austin in January 1901, Bailey was elected to the U.S. Senate, although not without opposition. The Speaker of the Texas House himself questioned whether he was too closely allied with Waters-Pierce Oil Company, which was liable to perpetrate "a fraud upon the State of Texas."

Bailey took the stand to repeat the statements that he made at the convention. In the end he prevailed, in all likelihood because there was no other credible candidate. He received 137 of the 141 votes cast. His bags were already packed. He left for Washington on the next train, hoping that the oil charter negotiation was a dead issue.

In the end, despite Hogg's best efforts, his campaigning, and his fervent hopes and prayers, William Jennings Bryan was defeated. With William McKinley in the White House, big business was in the saddle.

Bailey's first term in the Senate did not go as smoothly as he had hoped. In 1902 during a heated debate, he physically assaulted a fellow senator. His reputation was suspect thereafter. No longer did fellow senators look at him as a potential leader of the party.

Possibly Hogg might have repaired his fortunes enough to replace Bailey in 1906 if fate had not intervened.

In January 1905 James Hogg was injured in a train wreck on his way to Houston from Varner Plantation, the home he had managed to acquire with the money from Spindletop. His great bulk—at least three hundred pounds—was thrown to the floor and his neck was severely injured. The injury resulted in an abscess.

His health gradually deteriorated after that. In November he was to speak at a political rally for a gubernatorial candidate in Dallas. He reached Fort Worth but was too ill to continue to Dallas. Ima arranged for a recording to be made of his voice so it could be played in his place. Afterward he returned to Austin to the Driskill Hotel, where he remained for two months. During that time he came to believe he was not going to get well.

However, in February 1906, he was improved enough to go back to Varner where he seemed happy. He told his law partner Frank Jones, "I feel now that I am going to get well."

On Friday night, March 2, Texas Independence Day, he was visiting his partner. At midnight he went to bed. Jones went by his room at about eight o'clock the next morning and heard him breathing. He left orders that Hogg was not to be disturbed.

At eleven o'clock Ima knocked on his door and called, "Time for you to get up, Papa."

He was dead at age fifty-four. The politics of Texas suffered when he was no longer its guardian.

Did anyone appreciate the irony of his death? After his long political fight with Jay Gould and his opposition to the power of the railroads, he died as a result of a train wreck.

In 1906 a national magazine charged that Bailey was one of the senators who controlled the Senate to protect private interests at the expense of the public.

Perhaps the Texas congressmen had not read *Cosmopolitan*, or perhaps by that time too many owed too much to Waters-Pierce. Since no one stepped forward to challenge him, they re-elected him.

However, the oil scandal would not go away. Investigations early in Bailey's second term revealed that Waters-Pierce had never broken its ties with Standard Oil and was, in fact, part of the trust. The investigations also revealed the payments to Bailey as well as the personal loans with no indication that they had ever been repaid.

Bailey claimed later that the loans had never been made because he had rejected their efforts to buy him, but an investigation in 1907 revealed a paper with his signature in receipt of $3,000 for a "demand loan."

Water-Pierce's permit to do business in Texas was cancelled and penalties of $1,623,000 were assessed. In April 1909 the United States Supreme Court sustained the opinion. Waters-Pierce paid more than $1,718,000 in fines and interest. On December 7, 1909, the company's property in the state was sold for $1,431,741.78.

Bailey's public career was over as well. He resigned from the U.S. Senate, but—as before—he was never called to account for his deeds or misdeeds. He set up a lucrative law practice in Washington, D.C.

Perhaps he thought he could return to Texas in 1920 and everything would have been forgotten or forgiven. He came back to run for governor but was easily defeated. He established a law office in Dallas. He died nine years later during a trial in Sherman.

On May 31, 1913, with the passage of the Seventeenth Amendment, the people of Texas and the rest of the United States at last were allowed to vote for the senators who represent them.

"The Oilman as Politician"

Ross Shaw Sterling

"When I became governor, I was well-to-do, and now I return to the ranks of the poor from which I sprung."

Anything to Beat Ma Ferguson

Inevitably a few oil entrepreneurs came to realize that perhaps they might achieve more for their businesses if they actually sat in the chair of governance rather than buy the men who sat there. In 1930 those who controlled Texas politics had endured more than enough of Ma and Farmer Jim Ferguson. Ma looked frighteningly strong as her campaign for a second term gathered speed.

To forward the conservative agenda, Texas businessmen looked among themselves then looked far afield. Their eyes lighted on Ross Sterling, oilman, newspaperman, banker, former president of Humble Oil and Refining Company. Sponsored by big business and aided by most newspapers including those he owned, Sterling beat Ferguson by almost 100,000 votes in the Democratic primary runoff. The result of the general election was so much a certainty that only 300,000 people cared to vote.

With that mandate, Sterling should have had a successful term with the customary second term a foregone conclusion.

Instead, his term was an unmitigated disaster. The fact that the misery was caused almost totally by the Great Depression when it finally reached Texas was no excuse in the minds of most of her citizens. He was governor for only one term, beginning with such faith in the future in January 1931 and ending in humiliation in December 1933. His experience must have warned businessmen away, for Texas had very few to seek the office for a while.

Ross Sterling's formal education ended when he was thirteen years old. His mother died and he went to work in his father's feed store. He weighed 265 pounds and could carry a hundred-pound sack of feed under each arm. At twenty-eight, he went into business with his brother and sister. In 1903 he opened a feed store at the Sour Lake oil strike just west of Spindletop. His customers were the teamsters of the mule and oxen teams hauling heavy equipment to the next boomtown. He expanded to sell supplies to oil field operators. As Saratoga, Dayton, and Humble fields boomed in, Sterling opened more stores.

By the time a new store opened in Humble, north of Houston, he had enough money to buy an interest in two producing wells. In 1911 he organized the Humble Oil Company.

In 1917 he met two young men who got their start at Spindletop. They were wildcatters—not the ruthless wheeler-dealers of the movie screens—not the larger-than-life, go-for-broke, mean-as-a-polecat gamblers of the J. R. Ewing type portrayed by Larry Hagman. They were independent oilmen eager to form their own company. They and Sterling all had one thing in common—intelligence.

William S. Farish and R. L. Blaffer couldn't sell their oil for what they knew it was worth when the price of oil dropped to something ridiculous. They united to buck the "big boys" who controlled the pipelines and refineries that purchased their crude. They were a good fit for the feed store owner because he knew much of the business side of oil. When they joined his company, it became Humble Oil and Refining Company.

Young Farish had been a Mississippi lawyer. Blaffer's father owned a coal business in New Orleans. Joining the three was W. W. Fondren, a farmer's son who had come from Tennessee at seventeen with thirty cents in his pockets. He was such a humble man that even when he became president of the company, he still answered his own telephone.

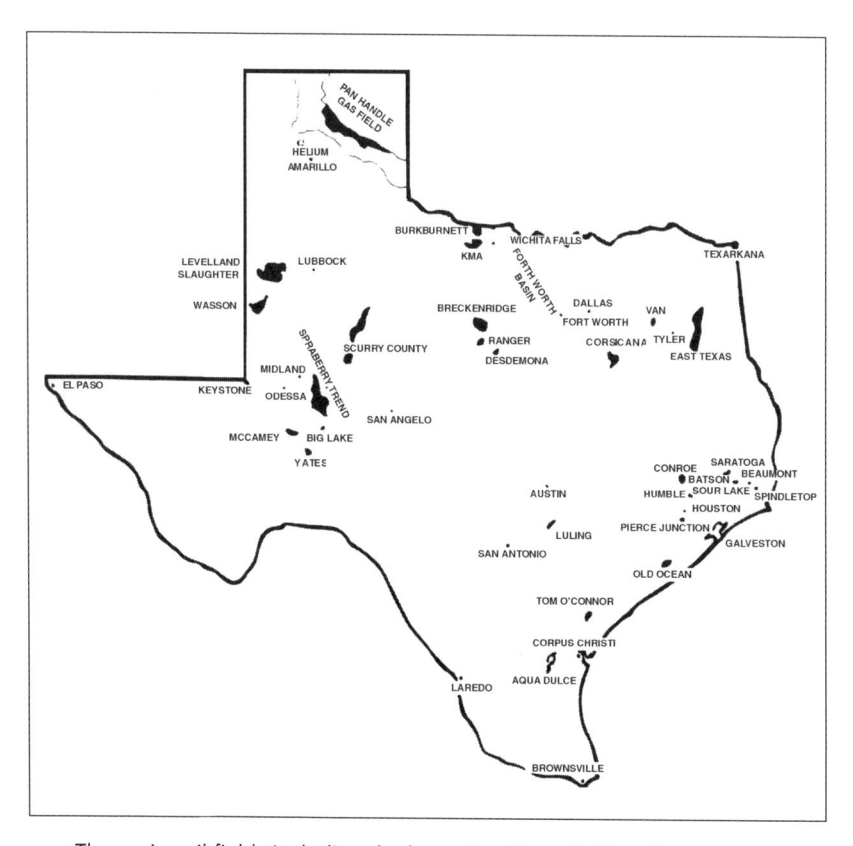

The major oil fields including the huge East Texas field and Spindletop. The number shown is only a few of the thousands of oil and gas fields drilled in Texas.

Completing the mix was Wallace Pratt, a geologist, who joined them later even though they weren't sure they needed one. They gave him the title chief geologist because he was the only one they had so, "Why not be chief of your own show?" With Ross Sterling as president of the company, they became a legend. Pratt predicted the fault line at Mexia thirty miles south and east of Corsicana, where the first Texas oil field had come in. Eventually, Pratt would go on to discover oil "where there was none" on the fabulous King Ranch in South Texas. They were highly successful and reasonably honest. "Buckskin Joe" Cullinan recommended them to anyone who asked.

Through World War I Farish worked on the Petroleum War Service Committee. If the terrible, senseless conflict proved nothing else, it proved the efficacy of oil as a motor fuel. Coal was eclipsed completely and has never regained its position. Electricity and gas found their niches elsewhere. As Lord Curzon remarked in 1920, "The Allies floated to victory on a wave of oil."

The gasoline-powered engine in the motorcar, which had been evolving slowly since 1900, now became the desirable mode of transportation. Horses were being replaced by something that didn't have to be fed unless a man used it. Hay cost more than gasoline. Why own a big, dumb animal when for $500 to $1,200, a family could own a Ford? Or a Packard? A Pierce-Arrow or a Stanhope? A Cadillac? A Rambler or a Locomobile?

In the meantime, the Texas legislature had become increasingly aware of the oil industry. In 1899 it passed the state's first petroleum conservation act. The act required that oil and gas wells be cased off to prevent the intrusion of water into the oil sand and conversely the intrusion of oil and gas into freshwater sand. It further provided for the plugging of all abandoned wells. It prohibited the escape of natural gas into the open air. The act was eminently sensible since *almost* everybody agreed that clean water and air were more important to the environment than oil.

In 1905 and 1913 statutes of similar nature were passed again with the idea of protecting the environment. The oil industry voiced almost no opposition. The legislature's toothless acts involved only the mechanics of drilling. They were in no way regulatory of either business or production. Furthermore, the politicians did not try to legislate drilling rights or ownership of the oil in the ground. The lawlessness that prevailed in the industry went on unabated.

The oil fields remained pockets of the wild, wild west in the midst of a Texas that was only slightly more civilized.

In 1917 came the most significant legislation of the decade—although no one in the oil industry recognized it. The legislature empowered James Hogg's Texas Railroad Commission to administer state petroleum conservation laws. The body established for the express purpose of regulating transportation in the state now had the power to regulate its natural resource.

An amendment to the Texas Constitution followed stating that "conservation and development of all of the natural resources of this State are *each and all* hereby declared public rights and duties, and the Legislature shall pass all such laws as may be appropriate thereto."

The question was asked contemptuously, "What did a trio of engineers know about oil?"

Neither oilmen nor railroad commissioners could guess what the amendment portended.

Meanwhile, so successful was the Humble Oil and Refining Company that it did not remain a Texas company for very long. James Hogg's old nemesis Standard Oil needed new blood.

Texas no longer had James Hogg to trumpet a warning.

The New Jersey branch of Rockefeller's monster proffered offers that no man among the young entrepreneurs could refuse. Though they resisted at first, they needed capital for expansion. In 1919 Humble sold half its stock for twenty million dollars, seventeen million of it in cash, to Standard. The moneys that exchanged hands were astronomical by World War I standards. In addition, Sterling, the president, sold some of his personal stock to the president of the New Jersey based company, Walter Teagle, who had to keep it separate and individual in order not to violate Texas law. Those in Texas and around the country who knew of the details of the sale realized that Sterling had sold his state down a river of oil to a trust bent on controlling the industry.

But something else was in the wind. Why did Standard pay so much for a company whose oil leases and wells were producing steadily rather than extravagantly? Many of their fields were actually about drilled out. Of course Standard wanted to get their feet back in Texas, where they'd missed several "black golden" opportunities. But still, they could have gotten better leases for less.

Ed Prather, an old Spindletop veteran, guessed the reason, thereby proving himself to be a prophet. "They aren't paying that much for any property," he opined. "They're paying for those boys! They don't have men like that up there. Before you and I die, those boys will be running the Standard Oil Company."

William Stamps Farish from Mississippi did indeed become president of Standard Oil.

Ross Sterling too would have been a big fat ace-in-the-hole for Standard had not the Great Depression interfered. After his big deal, the young man was a millionaire. He built a mansion in Houston, went into the lumber business, and acquired four banks. He also acquired the *Houston Dispatch* and the *Houston Post* and merged them into the *Houston Post-Dispatch,* which opposed Farmer Jim Ferguson's powerful manipulation of the Texas Highway Commission during his wife's first term in 1924.

Sterling's newspapers came out strongly against Ma Ferguson's re-election and were instrumental in helping Dan Moody defeat her. When Moody's term as governor was up, Sterling hired him to run the newspaper and took Moody's place on the ballot. Sterling had already dipped his toe into the political waters by being named chairman of the Texas Highway Commission. He ran for governor as "Your Big Fat Boy from Buffalo Bayou."

Sterling as the businessman's candidate promised a businesslike administration. Ma Ferguson, who had known nothing of business during her first term, had certainly not learned anything about it in preparation for her second.

Surprisingly, Texans were not prejudiced against him. Success in business has always been admired, perhaps because Texans admired the high-achiever, the loner who owes no man, the adventurer who succeeds in the face of tough odds. The rancher, the planter, and the independent oilman who earned their own successes are probably the most respected types in the state to this day.

As Dr. George Butte, University of Texas professor of the last decade, could have attested—the professional was never accorded the same respect. Dr. Butte was defeated by the "Old Gray Bonnet" in her successful first bid for election in 1924. When he proposed to run against Sterling and Ferguson in 1930, he polled only 5,001 votes in the Republican primary.

Nothing went right during Sterling's term. An ongoing drought plagued the state. Nationwide, a depression had dealt the whole country a fistful of very low cards. Though few Texans owned corporate stocks and bonds, they all depended on commodities. Farm prices were at an all-time low. Thousands of farmers were reduced to penury and evicted from their land. Banks who had lent money had no way to collect. Their operating capital was reduced to nothing. With no profits, no one could pay taxes.

Governor Ross Shaw Sterling made two fortunes in his lifetime. He found that governing the state was much different from conducting business. *Center for American Studies, UT-Austin*

With able-bodied men standing on street corners begging or camping out in hobo jungles, Sterling was forced to veto important relief legislation because state production was too low to implement it. The state treasury had no money and no prospects of raising any.

The worst and best thing that happened during his sad term in office was the appearance of two flamboyant ladies.

Their names were No. 3 Daisy Bradford and No. 1 Lou Della Crim.

East Texas Blows In

Columbus Marion Joiner was known far and wide as Dad. Grandad would have been more descriptive since he was sixty-seven years old. Like many farm boys born in 1860, he had almost no schooling (he claimed only seven weeks). He also claimed to be self-taught. He had read the Bible and Shakespeare, which he quoted frequently, thereby adding to his reputation. Born on an Alabama farm, he caught oil fever and went first to Oklahoma where he made and lost a fortune in the Indian lands.

Though he did drill wells, his strengths lay in promotion—interesting others in the gamble and selling them highly speculative leases. When his stock ran out in Oklahoma, he moved south to East Texas where in 1926 he had managed to lease four thousand acres. Very little money had changed hands in this deal. It was all speculative, and Joiner was deeply in debt.

One of the ironies of the oil business is that all wildcatters are essentially promoters until they strike. Then they become oilmen.

At about this time, Dad met up with a huge man who called himself Dr. A. C. Lloyd. "Doc" Lloyd weighed 320 pounds and

The odd couple. "Dad" Joiner shakes hands with "Doc" Lloyd. Fakers and confidence men at heart, through plain dumb luck they stumbled into the greatest oil discovery of the twentieth century.
Texas Mid-Continent Oil & Gas Association

stood six feet tall. Six years older than Joiner, he was even more a promoter than his partner. He was certainly more a promoter than the geologist he claimed to be.

He had claimed to be many things in his adventurous life. In Cincinnati where he was a drugstore clerk, his name was Joseph Idelbert Durham. When he worked for the federal government in Idaho, he was a chemist assaying gold. From there he became a mining engineer in the Yukon and then in Mexico. At one time he sold patent medicine as Dr. Alonzo Durham.

He also told that he had been married many times and fathered many children. The truth of that statement as well as many others is open to speculation.

He joined forces with Dad Joiner. In the famous photograph taken of the two shaking hands in front of Daisy Bradford No. 3, Joiner looks to be six inches shorter and 175 pounds lighter than the ponderous "Doc" Lloyd.

The odd couple's relationship soon turned into the laughingstock of the industry. True, Joiner had been able to lease an amazing number of acres of land for the small amount of capital he was believed to have, but its location was a joke. No oil had ever been thought of in that part of Texas. It didn't have salt domes or fault lines.

It was Piney Woods, for God's sake! People held their sides from laughing so hard.

The only thing that drew a bigger laugh was Lloyd's geologist's report. To begin with it was only two pages long. One page was a small outline map of the United States with locations of all the major oil fields: Signal Hill, Spindletop, and Bradford, Pennsylvania. Also noted were fields in Arkansas, Kansas, and Seminole, Oklahoma, where he and Joiner had met. From these various fields, lines were drawn in such a way that they intersected in East Texas.

In the last paragraph of the two-page written report, Dr. A. D. Lloyd averred, "All these major oil trends, intersecting as they do here in East Texas, bring about a state known in the oil business as the apex of the apex, a situation not found anywhere else in the world."

W. D. Hamm, who later became chief geologist for Atlantic-Richfield, was then district geologist in Ardmore, Oklahoma. When Joiner gave him the report to read, he had trouble keeping a straight face. Aloud, he wondered what in the world "apex of apex" meant. Knowing that the old man had been hoodwinked and hoping he hadn't paid anything for the "gibberish,"

Hamm told his secretary to say to Joiner that he didn't know anything good about it, but he didn't know anything bad about it either.

With that the old man went away satisfied. In August 1927 he spudded in a well on the widow Daisy Bradford's 975½-acre farm. Doc Lloyd avowed that Joiner was drilling in the wrong place, but Joiner had no choice. He had a lease for these acres, and he was going to bring the well in here. If the field was as big as Lloyd claimed, here would do as well as any.

No. 1 Daisy Bradford was the worst kind of operation. The rig was composed of scrap lumber and dilapidated machinery. The crew fueled its boilers with brushwood and discarded auto tires scavenged from the neighborhood. The drilling pipe was worn out, and Joiner had so little money that sometimes the drilling operation was shut down *except* on Sundays when investors drove over from Dallas to note the progress.

At 1,098 feet the bit jammed in the hole. All the work and all the precious pipe were lost. Nothing could be done except slide the rig a hundred feet aside and start No. 2 Daisy Bradford. By selling $25 certificates for a small interest in the well, Joiner got it down to two thousand feet before the pipe hung in the hole. The operation had to shut down again.

This time the old man made a trip to Houston for a new driller. Ed Laster came, looked at the wreck, and shook his head. "That pipe's hung in there in such a way we'll never be able to pull it out. You'll have to start a new well."

Dad shook his head. "That's more impossible than you think getting the pipe out is. I'll never be able to get folks to put up money for a third well."

Whether he felt sorry for the hopeful widow or whether his own optimism sustained him will never be known. The next day he spruced himself up and made the rounds with his $25 certificates. He sold them to waitresses, to post office clerks, to policemen, to storekeepers, and railroad workers. Every little man and woman in Rusk County had a piece of No. 3 Daisy Bradford.

In May 1929 they started drilling again.

No matter how the oil companies might snigger behind their hands, to the folks in Rusk County, Dad Joiner's well was their well too. They all had $25 certificates to prove it. When the drilling crew was short, farmers would quit their tasks and lend a hand for the day.

Walter D. Tucker, a banker in Overton, ten miles away, frequently drove over after the bank closed, donned overalls, and went to work. Mrs. Tucker cooked for the crew. When Dad couldn't pay the grocery bill, the Overton grocer accepted scrip on future production. He also let Dad use the back of his store for an office.

Dad issued so much scrip that the business of the town began to turn on it, and it was circulated like money as coal mining towns had done for over a century. The whole town became a great "company store."

The lease on Daisy Bradford's farm expired, but she gave Dad Joiner an extension and then another. She had faith in this well. The pathetic wreck had become the shining hope of people whose cotton had failed in '29 and '30. The swamp of the Great Depression was sucking them down. They were all praying for a gusher to blow them to the skies.

Dad wouldn't give up. He couldn't. Everyone was depending on him. He had never felt so responsible.

They had spent a year and four months drilling a 3,500-foot hole that should have taken only about six weeks. Every day something broke. The situation was desperate.

Then at about four o'clock one afternoon Ed Laster dropped a tester in the well—a long steel tube with sharp cutting teeth around its bottom edge. The process was a monotonous task since every joint of pipe that had been dragged out of the hole had to be swung over the hole again, screwed onto the joint below, and lowered.

At last on Laster's order the drill pipe began to rotate. The core barrel cut into the rock 3,536-feet down. The core of rock pushed up into the barrel. When it was filled, the clamps gripped the bottom of the core. The process was reversed.

When the test was pulled up, Laster at first saw nothing new. He emptied the core sample into two buckets sitting on the derrick floor. With the bottom of the core in the back of his pickup, he started to town. Only later when he examined the bottom of the core did he realize he was looking at nine inches of oil-saturated sand. At the same time he remembered that two buckets of the core were still sitting on the derrick floor.

He rushed back, but one bucket was missing.

One of the oil scouts, who were everywhere a well was being drilled, had stolen one of the buckets. The irony was that the oil scout later admitted the theft but told Laster he didn't believe the core. He thought Laster was salting it in the way miners salt their tailings with gold ore in an effort to lure new investors.

Still, enough people had seen the core to get an oil boom started—when there was no oil. People began trading leases. Dad Joiner was able to borrow money to drill deeper.

Somewhere a rumor began that No. 3 Daisy Bradford would come in October 1. By mid-morning eight thousand people swarmed around the well. Mrs. Bradford's young nephew sold a hundred cases of soft drinks. Candy, popcorn, and balloon vendors had a big day too.

But it wasn't the biggest day. On the morning of the third day, the crowd watched as Laster swabbed out the hole. It was a monotonous process. People grew restive, but nobody left.

Then late in the afternoon, a murmur ran through the crowd. Those closest to the well passed the information back over their shoulders that some oil was in the mud brought out by the swab.

A gurgling noise came from the pipe. Laster yelled at the crew to douse the boiler fire. Thousands of people—investors whose lives were riding on this well, their families, the curious, the scouts—all watched as a stream of oil began to spurt from the casing. It gathered volume and force as it rose higher and higher.

Oil and gas sprayed over the top of the derrick high enough for everyone among them to see.

The crowd shouted and laughed and wept. Men tossed their hats in the air and ran under the spray to take a shower bath. Children painted their faces with oil.

Dad Joiner was visibly shaken. "I always dreamed it, but I never believed it."

Two weeks later he was in court being sued by an impatient group of certificate owners who were afraid they wouldn't get their fair share of the profits.

The judge spoke for all East Texas when he said, "I believe that when it takes a man three and a half years to find a baby, he should be allowed to nurse it for a while. Hearing postponed indefinitely."

By that time Joiner was seventy years old. He had no capital. He had no education to handle the string of lawsuits and the tangle of litigation his promotions had generated. In a month he asked for voluntary receivership. With a sigh of relief, he sold his well and the acreage surrounding it and some four thousand acres of undisputed leases for $30,000 cash and the promise of royalties in the amount of $1,500,000.

The man who bought it was a thirty-one-year-old professional gambler from Arkansas. No one at that time knew how big the field was. No one knew how much oil would come out of it. Despite the oil being pumped out of the ground before their eyes, the geologists continued to insist that it was just a flash well. There really wasn't any oil to speak of. The gambler would lose his shirt.

Only a real gambler would take those odds along with a snake-pit of lawsuits. A professional gambler. He was Haroldson Lafayette Hunt.

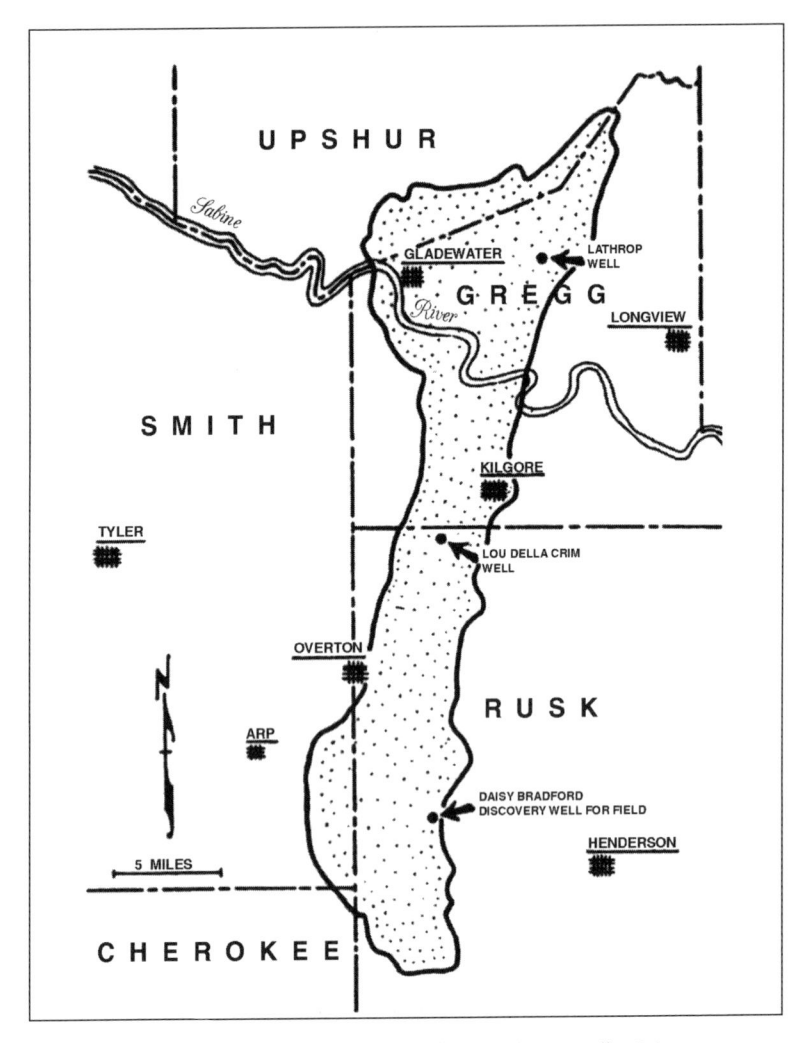

The flaming ladies—Daisy Bradford and Lou Della Crim.
The East Texas lake of oil spread under five counties.

The Hot Oil War

The cold November day before H. L. Hunt bought Dad Joiner's properties, Ed Bateman, a Fort Worth newspaperman turned wildcatter, spudded in a well on Mrs. Lou Della Crim's 900-acre farm at Kilgore, *twelve miles north* of Rusk. On December 28, 1930, the No. 1 Lou Della Crim came roaring in. Estimates ran has high as 22,000 barrels a day.

East Texas went wild. Within a few weeks the entire town of Kilgore sprouted derricks.

And it wasn't over.

In Longview, twelve miles north of Kilgore, the Chamber of Commerce offered $10,000 for the first well in the town's trade area. Only twenty-eight days after Kilgore, J. A. Moncrief, another wildcatter, and the Arkansas Fuel Company working jointly brought in a huge producer five miles northeast of the town.

All these wells were producing from the Woodbine Sand. In a matter of weeks one huge producing well after another was being brought in in ever-widening circles from the three original wells. No one in the country—perhaps in the entire world—was prepared for the magnitude of the field. East Texas was soon producing over an area of 211 square miles. A forest of derricks forty-three miles long and three to twelve miles wide stretched over East Texas.

The gigantic field was the making of more fortunes and more independent oil companies than any other field in history. It also ushered in the familiar cycle of flush production and falling prices.

At Spindletop, where many of the major Texas oil producers got their start, they had been able to control the amount of oil pumped. When the East Texas field blew in, the wildcatters literally went wild. The field was too big, the amount of acreage that could be leased too vast for even the big companies to control it. The independents were drilling wells left and right, striking oil at almost every shaft and trying to sell it.

Texas had witnessed disastrous falling prices in 1901 at Spindletop. The state could not afford another such disaster. Early in 1930 James Hogg's Texas Railroad Commission assumed power over oil production based on their ability to regulate anything that moved by any process—rail, highway, barge, or pipeline—across state lines. They issued an order for proration of drilling on each well.

In February 1930 the Independent Petroleum Association of Texas (IPAT) was organized in Fort Worth. Its purpose was war. Its offensive was two-pronged. First was to oppose in every way it could the major oil companies who its members rightly believed were trying to squeeze out the little man. Second was to resist the prorationing Ross Sterling, himself an oilman, and his "damned" railroad commission were trying to push on them.

"Prorationing" was a dirty word, anathema to wildcatters' ears. To them it sounded like big business trying to keep their profits down and squeeze them out. They reasoned that if petroleum production from a common reservoir or source was to be restricted by the Texas Railroad Commission, the commission would take the advice of the lawyers the major producers were able to afford.

Since the East Texas field was clearly a single source, the duty assumed by the commission was to assign "allowables"—maximum quantities of oil to be produced. These allowables would be assigned per field, per lease within the field, and per well within the lease.

The commission was to meet once a month to assess the going market demand for Texas oil and keep production at that level. More maddening was the extension of the commission's duties to include regulation of production as follows:

1. Issue drilling permits after a study of each application in its relation to other wells in the area.
2. Inspect each well at completion as to equipment, safety, and problems related to physical waste.
3. Regulate production to conform to market demand.
4. Set allowables in accordance with formulas prescribed in individual field rules and keep records of crude-oil production.

IPAT howled. If a man only had one or two leases with two or three wells per lease, he wouldn't be able to make the money that Humble, Texaco, Gulf, and Standard would with hundreds of leases, thousands of wells. This whole idea of prorationing was aimed straight at competition.

Still, in the face of falling oil prices, the oil producers, both independent and incorporated, made a lame effort at self-regulation. If that failed, then prorationing was the only possible solution apart from declaring martial law as Governor Bill Murray had done in Oklahoma.

The price of oil dropped from a dollar a barrel to ten cents a barrel. On one occasion, one million barrels of Texas crude were sold for $25,000—2½ cents a barrel. The motorists were delighted to buy gasoline for seven or eight cents a gallon, but cheap East Texas oil was closing down fields and stopping production all over America.

The entire industry was rushing toward a gigantic train wreck.

The pressure from outside Texas was intense. Sterling with his background in oil understood what was happening economically and also ecologically. A natural resource of the people of Texas was being wasted. Hundreds of wells were drilled, depleting this gigantic field to capture the *ferae naturae* that lay only a few thousand feet below the Piney Woods.

Subsidiary industries grew up overnight. Entrepreneurs came in to lay pipelines from the wells to the equally entrepreneurial "teakettle" refineries that sprang up to separate the gasoline from the oil. Because of the quality of the crude from the East Texas lake, refining was just as cheap and easy as drilling.

When the field was discovered, oil was selling for $1.10 a barrel. By June 1931 the thousand completed wells in East Texas were producing 360,000 barrels a day—15,120,000 gallons of sweet Texas crude. As one operator complained, "Hell, I sell a barrel of oil for ten cents and a bowl of chili costs me fifteen."

Something had to be done. In August twelve hundred sane souls calling themselves the East Texas Chamber of Commerce signed a petition requesting that production be stopped. Sterling Ross had the unenviable task of doing it. August 17, 1931, he sent the National Guard into East Texas to shut down the wells that by that time were producing 848,000 barrels a day.

"Here Comes The Law!"

On August 17 at 6 A.M. Ross Sterling, the man who had made a fortune in oil, sent troops into the East Texas field. General Jacob Wolters took 99 officers and 1,104 enlisted men to Kilgore to control about 1,600 wells. While soldiers patrolled on horseback night and day and National Guard airplanes flew overhead, the drilling went on with hardly a ripple. Far from making a difference, the presence of Wolters under orders from Sterling only exacerbated the problems.

Wolters was Texaco's general counsel, and his aide was a Gulf official. Sterling was believed to have acted strictly for the benefit of the large oil companies. In all likelihood he did, but he really had little choice. At least Wolters knew what to look for. In that respect his choice was a logical one.

Wolters found he couldn't control the situation. He was sent to shut down old wells. Since new wells could be drilled for about $32,000 in three and a half weeks, the wildcatters simply slid their operations to one side (as Dad Joiner had done with Daisy Bradford Nos. 1 and 2) and brought in another well to capture the oil from a new well right under the general's nose.

Some operators simply set up dummy derricks beside the ones in operation, pretended to drill during the daytime, and operated at night from the original well, running the oil through underground pipe to the dummies. It was a dangerous enterprise because thieves discovered they could rob the night crews with impunity because the men engaged in illegal activity could not report the crimes.

Another favorite tactic of "hot oilers" was to drill a slant hole. Drillers had long known that if a "straight" hole deviated as little as three degrees from perpendicular it could bottom anywhere within seven acres.

Careless, inexperienced wildcatters had sometimes gotten their lines tangled underground when they drilled on a hillside. Now new wells could be drilled acres away from proven sites and bring in wells from underground.

The deviousness grew and grew as techniques developed that would later prove invaluable in drilling under lakes and rivers. A well could be drilled straight for several thousand feet and then slanted. Incidentally, drilling on the offshore ice in the polar regions in winter, completing the well, and then setting up an offshore drilling operation may be the solution to drilling under the Arctic Wildlife Refuge.

Bootleggers of Arkansas moonshine had run their cars and pickups loaded with quart jars and jugs filled with "white lightning" over the back roads in the dead of night, sometimes with the lights turned off. Just so bootleg oil ran at night through secret buried lines to refineries and pipeline buyers who kept no record of their amounts. New wells had real and dummy pipelines dug at the same time to handle both legal and illegal product.

Tank trucks carrying anywhere from 500 to 1,000 gallons of gasoline rolled out of the teakettle refineries at night. A man willing to take the risk of driving the highly flammable stuff could earn a hundred dollars if he could get his load to Dallas or Houston.

Lawlessness inevitably bred lawlessness. The "underworld characters" made traveling the backroads and state and county highways after dark a dangerous enterprise. It was too easy to hop on the running boards or into the back of pickups and trucks and force the driver to stop and get out. Sometimes they would threaten him with a gun. Sometimes a lighted match was sufficient. The air was full of the fumes from gasoline. If the driver was lucky, he got to run for his life.

Three men drove into the Guard camp at Kilgore in the dead of night, shot at the soldiers (presumably fellow Texans), and then drove away when the soldiers returned fire.

Wherever wild men are making money, wild women will come to help them spend it. At 2:30 A.M. a Kilgore attorney was awakened to arrange bail for twenty-five naked women arrested during a raid on a dancehall called the "Midnight Rambler." The jails in all the small towns housed prostitutes on a regular basis.

The *Gladewater Gusher,* a fly-by-night rag, accused Sterling of high treason and called for his impeachment. It blamed everything on the governor and big oil. Fortunately, the *Gusher* died before the army was recalled. East Texas was shut down for nineteen days although drilling from "new" wells continued.

The Texas Ranger sent to Kilgore was one of the most flamboyant of that colorful breed. Sergeant Manuel T. "Lone Wolf" Gonzaulles rode into town on his shiny black horse. The sun glinted off the pair of pearl handled pistols strapped to his waist. A wag is supposed to have yelled, "Here comes 'The Law'!"

Lone Wolf was probably the most feared and respected man in Texas at that time. Trading on his fearsome reputation, he exercised his full authority to play judge, jury, and jailer to the criminals. The fact that Kilgore lacked a jail didn't stop him. In quick order he began making arrests. At first he handcuffed his prisoners to a big oak tree, but as the number grew, he realized he had to make other arrangements. When his arrests grew to more than three hundred men, he chained them and marched them to a local Baptist church that had been vandalized. Fastening them in front of the church, he displayed, identified them, and fingerprinted them.

The sight was called "Lone Wolf's Trotline." The local joke was, "Lone Wolf gave the misfits four hours to get out of town and they gave three hours and fifty minutes of it back to Lone Wolf."

Meanwhile, the Railroad Commission met and limited production to 225 barrels per well. The price climbed to eighty-three cents, but the operators brought lawsuits because they couldn't break even on that allowance.

All these efforts came to naught but a drop in the bucket.

Because of the number of wells, the associated gases were being burned off. Millions of gallons were being left in the ground as pressure dropped with no possibility of recovery. The result was depletion on an unheard-of scale. Moreover, the leases spread over 140,000 acres in parts of the five counties of Upshur, Smith, Gregg, Rusk, and Cherokee were impossible to police. Every sort of criminal activity was being carried on among the 32,000 wells located among the dark pines miles from the little towns equally at the mercy of depredations. One reporter wrote, "The East Texas highways... [are]... almost as exciting as a Chicago street during the gang wars."

As National Guard Sergeant D. W. Johnson was checking tanks near Gladewater one night, a cold cutting wind blew rain into his numbed face. He complained about the weather to the man watching the lease.

"Just lean up against a tank of that oil," the man suggested. "It's hot enough to keep you warm."

Even worse in the minds of many Texans was Sterling's sending the Texas Rangers and the National Guard into the East Texas oilfields ostensibly to control runaway oil production, which had become a national issue. In reality Texas Ranger Manuel T. "Lone Wolf" Gonzaulles was sent to quell the countless lawless acts that included robbing the work crews on the oilrigs, thereby curtailing production.

Even "Lone Wolf" could not bring the oil fields under control. Sterling was forced to declare martial law. As of 6 A.M. on August 17, 1931, all oil wells in Gregg, Rusk, Smith, and Upshur Counties were shut down.

Even that situation would not last. Hot oil continued to run as freely as ever. In October Jack D. Wrather, who owned a refinery in Kilgore, obtained a federal injunction that prohibited the Railroad Commission, the attorney general, the county attorney, and General Wolters from interfering with oil production. Immediately, Wrather returned to pumping 5,000 barrels per well daily.

Insisting that the injunction applied only to Wrather's five wells, Sterling assumed the authority to prorate the entire field. The order was futile. No one could control East Texas, especially when money was talking to Washington legislators who in turn were talking to federal judges.

In the spring of 1932, the federal courts permanently enjoined Sterling from enforcing proration. He appealed the case to the United States Supreme Court. In the meantime, the depression sank its claws deep into Texas. Times were hard; temptations were great; the Piney Woods were dark and deep.

The "peace officers," as the National Guardsmen were then titled by Sterling, continued to pursue the hot oil runners, but their hearts weren't in their jobs. One special investigator was peppered with birdshot. A well belonging to one of the major oil companies was dynamited.

Sterling had done all he could. The people of Texas hated him for it. He lost the primary election to Ma Ferguson, running for her second term. Her weapons were Sterling's handling of the East Texas field and his vetoing of state aid to destitute families.

On December 12, 1932, the Supreme Court ruled that Sterling's enforcement of proration with troops was illegal. After sixteen months martial law was finally over. The fate of East Texas and ultimately the rights of states to regulate much of their own business passed into the hands of the federal government.

Within six months, with East Texas oil worth four cents a barrel, Governor Miriam Ferguson telegraphed Harold L. Ickes, Franklin Delano Roosevelt's new Secretary of the Interior. In the wire she admitted that the situation was beyond the control of state authorities and pleaded for stringent federal legislation.

A joke was told over and over as the situation worsened and the depression affected every walk of Texas life:

> A sadly depressed independent oilman sought comfort in a small church in East Texas. The proration battle had taken all his strength. He'd been out late the night before running hot oil through an illegal pipeline. He dozed off shortly after the beginning of the sermon.
>
> Suddenly he jerked awake, as the preacher begged the Heavenly Father, "Oh, Lord. Bless the Pure and Humble."
>
> "Hold on there, parson!" The oilman jumped to his feet. "Us independents are still in this fight, and I want you to put in a word for us."

Sterling returned to private life although not to the Humble Oil and Refining Company, which eventually became Esso (for Standard Oil), then Exxon, then Exxon-Mobil, the largest oil company in the world. He remade his fortune in the Sterling Oil and Refining Company and was known in his last years for his philanthropy.

The Hot Oil War Goes National

The Governor at Bay—James V Allred

The waste of natural resources and the failure of the general population to obey the laws in East Texas was more than a Texas scandal and a disgrace. It became a national disaster whose tremors stretched far beyond the magnitude of the Chicago fire, the Galveston hurricane, or the San Francisco earthquake.

In subtle and not-so-subtle ways, it affected the entire United States in terms of loss of energy forever, in terms of family finances strained for years, in terms of industrial recovery slowed and human misery extended. It resulted in hard times for the economies in all the oil producing fields and the shutting down of some fields entirely. All the workers and their families were adversely affected as well as the businesses in the towns and counties in which they worked.

Occurring in the depths of the Great Depression brought on by the stock market collapse and the failure of banks nationwide, it changed forever the *laissez-faire* attitude of even the most conservative members of government. The legislature and the president were caught flat-footed with no measures in place to alleviate the suffering. It paved the way for the socially conscious liberalism that exists today.

If Lyndon Johnson's Great Society had its roots in the Great Depression, its taproot stretched even deeper—more than 3,500 feet down into East Texas. So outrageous was the situation that oilmen, as well as public officials who in many cases were in their pockets, were forced to face the fact that existing laws stood no chance of dealing with the problems of petroleum.

Ordinary citizens and small town governments were helpless. Local law enforcement and state militia were a joke. "Government by the consent of the governed" took on a whole new meaning.

At the same time, Texans were afraid. Martial law was the death knell to the spirit of the westering daredevils who had pioneered the state. Sam Houston and Stephen F. Austin had fought for independence. They could never have foreseen such a world of outlaws as the twentieth-century wildcatters.

To give most of the governors of Texas their due, they tried to hold back federal regulation. Rightly, they recognized that any power the federal government took upon itself would never be returned to the states. Moreover, they recognized from their own fumbling experiments that a law passed for the very best of reasons frequently backfired or had unexpected and unpleasant consequences.

First among the governors to try to forestall federal takeover was James V Allred, who succeeded Ma Ferguson at the end of her second term in 1935. A naval veteran of World War I, who maintained the V in his name stood for nothing, he studied law and became a "fighting district attorney."

The situation was so extreme toward the end of Ferguson's term that she begged Roosevelt to take over control of the Texas oil fields. Then in desperation she closed the banks statewide three days before Roosevelt did nationwide.

Meanwhile, the president consulted with his New York friends and associates and learned that, not surprisingly,

The Hot Oil War Goes National

Standard Oil was in favor of federal regulation. Rockefeller's fields had all felt the pinch of East Texas excess. With that mandate, Roosevelt was ready to name an "oil czar," who would have federal authority to prorate oil production. He was more than irritated when a Texas congressman, young Sam Rayburn, chairman of the House Committee on Interstate and Foreign Commerce, forestalled the appointment.

In 1934 Ferguson chose not to run. Perhaps a sense of her own inadequacies in the face of mounting suffering among the farm families she had championed so long influenced her decision. Still not out of politics, she and Pa put up their own candidate, C. C. McDonald. A measure of how disenchanted her voters were with her is the fact that McDonald did not even make the primary runoff.

Allred, who came in first, promised the voters that he would act as a governor should to control East Texas. When he won the election, though he was a conservative at heart, he nevertheless used the Texas Planning Board to institute several federal programs aimed at relief for struggling families.

Most important to national interests was his cooperation with Governor Marland of Oklahoma to form a governing body of states to control oil. Texas, Oklahoma, California, and the rest of the oil states were by that time making inroads to control their individual production. Only East Texas, because of its great size, resisted Allred's best efforts.

Still, oil operators themselves had begun to realize that they were ruining, not bettering themselves, by flouting regulations. Saner heads were at last prevailing even among the wildcatters.

Hot oil runners protested that they were just trying to support their families, but their time had come. By 1935 relief and reforms were in effect. On January 22 the Congress of the United States passed the Connally Hot Oil Act, written by none other than Senator Tom Connally of Texas. It had once and for all defined "illegal petroleum" as "crude oil produced or withdrawn from storage in violation of state allowables." It was further a felony offense to ship it in interstate or foreign commerce.

Not quite a month later, Allred called a meeting of the nine heads of the oil producing states to put together the Interstate Oil Compact Commission. By doing so they hoped to retain their states' rights to regulate the resources within them and to bring to justice those who violated their laws. The punishment of hot oil runners would *not* be under federal jurisdiction.

Roosevelt's Secretary of the Interior Harold Ickes was opposed to the compact because "no state can regulate interstate commerce" or protect itself from another state. He argued that crude oil was a natural resource belonging to all the American people. It was important to the national security. Therefore, it should be a matter for the federal government. The fight for control was on. Independents as well as in-state companies recognized their industry was in danger of trading Standard Oil for the Federal Bureau of Investigation.

While Ickes kept up recommendations and demands for federal regulation of the oil industry, Roosevelt backed off. Pending in Congress was his huge reform package that would change forever labor relations, banking, and the most revolutionary of all—social security. He could not afford to anger Texas, California, Oklahoma, et cetera, almost all of whom voted Democratic.

Since timing is everything, the oilmen got lucky. They contributed to a war chest to hire a battalion of lawyers to oppose federal control. "The oil industry is prepared to do its part...if it can know clearly that its efforts are not to be checkmated by constant change, bureaucratic dictation, or usurpation of power."

The Hot Oil War Goes National

Governor James V Allred with his family. His youth and enthusiasm as well as his credentials offered voters a real change from Ma Ferguson.
Center for American History, UT-Austin

In the end the Connally Hot Oil Act was some of the most conservative legislation to come out of Roosevelt's administration. Ratified by Congress on August 22 and the Senate on the 24th, it permitted each state to enforce its own oil production regulations.

In the meantime, science had at last been able to catch up with the oil industry. Texas Railroad Commissioner Ernest O. Thompson had all the wells in East Texas (close to 2,000) tested. The survey showed that the field could produce 100 million barrels a day. By a conservative estimate that was twenty-six times more than the entire world could consume in the same period.

The tests also showed that there was such gas waste from the thousands of unnecessary wells drilled to take advantage of the law of capture that unless production was slowed, billions of barrels would be unrecoverable. The constant scientific improvements in the industry as well as the discovery of nearly all the "shallow" deposits had taken oil drilling beyond the luck and brawn of the wildcatters to brains and their resulting science.

William Farish, who had moved with Humble into the Standard Oil empire, remembered his roots. He called for adequate laws "requiring the performance of those things which science and engineering have found to be essential to conservation, to efficient oil production, and to the protection of the correlative rights of the common owners of an oil pool."

While a few old wildcatters howled, almost everybody agreed that the time had come for the "law of capture" to be consigned to the dustbin. Vice president of Sun Oil J. Edgar Pew led the charge by reminding everyone that wild game was subject to hunting seasons, licenses, and leases. In other words, it was preserved rather than hunted out and destroyed altogether.

Oil had to be preserved just as deer and ducks.

At the same time he did not want to ruthlessly crush the "splendid forces of adventure, initiative, individual effort, and bull-necked courage on which the industry depends for finding the hidden stores."

The governors maintained that traditional understandings of the laws of supply and demand were not truly applicable to the oil industry. Prorationing would not work if government arbitrarily applied it. Market-supply prorationing was the new watchword.

Still Allred and the other governors disagreed. Allred was a special friend of Roosevelt, who admired young lawyers with intelligence and spirit. Most important to Roosevelt was the fact that when Allred came up for re-election, he polled fifty-two percent of the majority in the Democratic primary and, of course, swept the state in the general election. The people of Texas had spoken.

More important, science had spoken. The unrestrained drilling stopped. Some overnight; some gradually. The price of oil climbed again as *less* became worth *more*.

One final analysis is the proof of the wise use of natural resources: Had conservation not gone into effect in the East Texas field, it would have finally yielded one billion barrels of oil. It is now seventy years old and has yielded six billion barrels of oil with an estimated one billion barrels still to be produced. When the field has been depleted, eighty-six percent of the oil will have been recovered.

In the end as Texans had hoped, East Texas has saved herself.

Because of Allred's obvious influence, Roosevelt withheld the executive order that would have placed the oil fields under federal regulation. Late in his second term in 1938, Roosevelt nominated the still youthful governor for a federal district judgeship. In 1949 Harry Truman appointed him to the Fifth

Texas Politicians: Good 'n' Bad

Franklin Delano Roosevelt liked young smart men. Two of the smartest were James V Allred in his second term as governor and young congressman-elect Lyndon Baines Johnson. Roosevelt's New Deal brought a host of such men into power and prominence all across the country.
Austin-American Statesman

Circuit Court of Appeals, where he remained until his death in 1959.

Allred's career exemplifies the politician who could play the game to perfection. In every case he chose the winning side. When the rights of states and the individuals gave him an advantage, he summoned all his resources to organize them. In so doing he was able to exert power over the president of the United States by having a huge block of votes at his disposal.

Altogether, Allred's two terms can be said to be a success.

While he used his bully pulpit to convince Texans that the national recovery program was a good thing, he wasn't able to get the legislature (a much, much more conservative body) to fund the program's services. The legislators were willing to pass a teacher retirement system, to advocate more educational programs, to vote salary increases including the governor's from $4,000 to $12,000 per year, and to broaden social security and welfare programs. Votes *for* such programs were good to take home to the voters.

Votes for funding for such programs involved tax increases. Those were not good to take home to voters. Legislators from poorer counties could not in good conscience add to their people's burdens. They were therefore unwilling to provide additional revenues such as a state sales tax to pay for the services.

Fortunately, under Roosevelt's New Deal, Texas was able to transfer approximately seventy percent of its social costs to the federal government. Thus the strings were attached that would turn to lines of attack on private property and social organization in the not-too-distant future.

Corporate capitalism took the blame when it passed on its added tax burdens to the people. Those whose homes and farms were threatened remained oblivious to the reason behind the rise in prices and voted, as ever, enthusiastically Democratic.

During World War II, Secretary of the Interior Ickes had the last word in controlling the amount of oil pumped in East Texas. At his suggestion a twenty-four-inch-diameter pipe was laid to the refining centers of the northeast rather than allowing Texans to refine and ship their own oil. Built by a consortium of U.S. oil companies as a means of getting the oil safely and efficiently to fuel the war in the European Theatre of Operations, it was deemed a patriotic necessity.

During World War II the East Texas oil field produced more oil than the Axis powers combined. Again America floated to victory on a lake of oil.

The Tide Turns—Robert Allan Shivers

From the first, Allan Shivers was a comer. He never seemed to put a foot wrong. After completing high school at Port Arthur in 1924, he went to study law at the University of Texas but dropped out after a year to work in the oil refinery in his hometown. For three years he was associated in the most elemental way with the most vital industry in the state. In 1934 he earned his law degree, set up his practice the next year, and was elected to the Texas State Senate at age twenty-seven, the youngest member ever to sit in that body. In 1937 he married Marialice Shary, the daughter of John H. Shary, a citrus grower, cattleman, banker, and realtor in the Rio Grande Valley. Her family was his entrée into the world of the Texas rich and powerful. He had married very well for himself.

During World War II he served two and a half years with the army from North Africa to Germany where he attained the rank of major with five battle stars and the Bronze Star. Returning a war hero, he ran for and won the office of lieutenant governor. When the governor, Beauford Jester, died, Shivers became the state's leader.

The Hot Oil War Goes National

Allan Shivers took the battle for the tidelands to the Democratic National Convention. He was the only governor in Texas history to win the state in both the Republican and Democratic primaries.
Center for American Studies, UT-Austin

His appeal to Texans was his great asset. He was as tough as any man among them and as political a man as has ever held the office. A contemporary photograph, perhaps snapped while he was unaware, perhaps posed for, shows him leaning back at ease in a Stetson, a checkered shirt with pearl stud buttons, and a tooled leather belt with a fancy buckle. He is in the act of rolling his own cigarette as he looks sidewise off camera at someone. His expression is quizzical. His eyes have the searching steely look of a Western hero.

He stood six-feet-two with a military bearing. He used his commanding presence to great advantage. More important he was a man possessed of great good sense who understood that a governor must be the great promoter of legislation. As he often maintained, "The popular image of governorship, if not tarnished by the incumbent's own actions, is a potent asset in politics."

One of his most famous speeches said in part:

"Texas, the proud Lone Star State—first in oil—forty-eighth in mental hospitals. [There were only forty-eight states at that time.]

"First in cotton—worst in tuberculosis.

"First in raising goats—last in caring for state wards."

If timing was everything, then Allan Shivers was Texas's best man for the time. He was the ideal town marshal to take the walk down the dusty main street to face the interloper.

In 1948 Harry S Truman had won the presidency over Thomas E. Dewey, the Republican candidate. One of the most controversial issues in the campaign was who owned the land offshore. In 1949 a statewide opinion poll reported that Texans were most concerned about retaining their tidelands.

By 1950 the major onshore oil reserves in Texas had been discovered although much had not been developed and much was being conserved. But offshore lay untold wealth, most within reasonably easy reach. For the first time coastal states became concerned about this important source of their income procured in the form of leases. Millions of dollars poured into their treasuries from corporations that retrieved not just oil, but kelp, shell, sand, marl, and fish. Other corporations constructed ports, docks, and piers where shipping from all over the world unloaded and loaded cargoes.

Unfortunately, the United States government charged much less for federal leases, so oil companies were behind the federal officials one hundred percent when they asserted national ownership to the seacoast of California. Coastal states knew that their rights to lands and leases would follow in short order. People were incensed.

While all along the Pacific and Atlantic coastlines and two-thirds of the Gulf of Mexico, people were cursing and gnashing their teeth, Texans remained cool. They were sure they held a fistful of aces.

Their submerged land in the Gulf of Mexico between low tide and the state's boundary was more than three times larger than other states. It amounted to 2,440,650 acres extending out 10.35 miles into the Gulf, the distance of three Spanish leagues. Suddenly, everyone was reading the contract of 1845 by which Texas had been annexed by the United States.

President Andrew Jackson himself had read the Texas Declaration of Independence to the Joint Session of the United States Congress in 1837: "beginning at the mouth of the Sabine river, and running West along the Gulf of Mexico, three leagues from land. The title of Texas to territory she claims is identified with her independence."

The Annexation Agreement of 1845 and the Treaty of Guadalupe Hidalgo of 1848 ending the Mexican War had both cited the three leagues boundary.

When the federal government needed sites for lighthouses, fortifications, and jetties in the Gulf areas, it had obtained grants for sites from the Texas legislature and paid handsomely

Texas Politicians: Good 'n' Bad

for them. In the same manner, Texas as well as other coastal states had leased mineral rights for offshore activities to the highest bidders.

When the federal government granted itself the right to lease such spots, they charged twenty-five cents per acre for undeveloped land. The outrage reached epic proportions. This was not one one-hundredth of the price per acre averaged by the states. Almost immediately, over a thousand federal lease applicants blanketed the coasts of Texas, California, and Louisiana. Worse was the fact that these applications were for leases already covered by state leases.

The amount Texas stood to lose was a whopping $10 million annually in bonus revenues. All Texas public lands were kept in trust as a source of revenue for the public school fund. The federal government was trying to take books out of the hands of schoolchildren. Rancor ran high.

And with it ran fear. The loss was as threatening as an oncoming train.

The first federal lawsuit asserted federal ownership to land held by the United States before California became a state. It held that therefore California had never owned her offshore lands, and the ruling that she had had been erroneous. Texas Attorney General Price Daniel and all the other states attorneys general filed an *amicus curiae* brief in opposition to the federal claim.

State after state climbed on the bandwagon to protect themselves as they saw federal encroachment of waterways, rivers, and lakes as the next logical step. In 1946 in response to the outcry of its constituents, Congress passed a bill recognizing and confirming state ownership of the property, but President Harry Truman vetoed it.

When the matter was finally brought before the Supreme Court, the split decision was shocking and frightening. It was also one of the most criticized opinions in the history of the

Court. Justice Hugo Black agreed that the states had possessed the soils under navigable waters and that the federal government had agreed with them—but with the discovery of oil and other property necessary to national defense and the conduct of international affairs, "mere property ownership" was an insufficient reason for their *keeping* the offshore lands. "The United States here asserts rights in two capacities transcending those of a mere property owner."

The ruling allowed the government to confiscate property in the national interest. Where was freedom? Where was justice?

Why the federal government so ruled is open to speculation. The possibility of another world war with Russia influenced the Justices. Fear of the "Communist menace" was everywhere. Spies were known to have given the Soviet Union America's ultimate weapon—the atomic bomb. Certainly, President Harry Truman had no illusions or compunction as to what should be done in wartime. He had risen through the ranks to major and battalion commander during World War I. He was also the only man in the history of the world to order two atomic bombs to be dropped on civilian cities.

He would certainly have had no problem exercising federal "paramount right and power" to take oil and other property without ownership and without compensation. While the whole of the United States stood aghast at what the decision meant to them, Texas retained hope that she would be allowed to keep her lands because she had a special title because of the Annexation Agreement.

The worst betrayal was yet to come.

During his presidential campaign Harry Truman spoke in Austin in August 1948 declaring, "Texas is in a class by itself." Even Harold Ickes, the former Secretary of the Interior and a champion of the fight against state ownership of anything said

Texas Politicians: Good 'n' Bad

on national television, "Texas may have the legal right to its tidelands."

Dangled a carrot, Texas went Democratic in the election as she had always done. Within months she was to learn about "political promises and piecrusts."

Shortly after the general election, Truman handed down an executive order. Attorney General Tom Clark (a Dallas attorney who had stated to the press in 1947 that Texas "as a Republic owned all of the lands... including... [the]... tidelands.") filed suit against the state. He further made a motion for a summary judgment without a hearing. Though Texas made a strong plea, the Supreme Court voted four to three against her. For the first time in the Court's history, a state was denied the right to introduce evidence.

While everyone was reeling, Texas moved for a rehearing. While it was allowed, it proved to be a waste of time. The Court did not change its decision.

In 1952 Congress again passed a bill restoring to the states the title to all submerged lands. President Truman vetoed it again. "Give 'em Hell, Harry," was living up to his name.

But Truman would not be president after 1952. On February 26, 1951, the Twenty-Second Amendment to the Constitution stated that no one could be elected to the office of president more than twice, and no man acting as president for more than two years could be elected more than once thereafter. Though the amendment had been written in such a way as to allow Truman his second term, the sixty-eight-year-old Missourian had already sworn to abide by the new law of the land.

Texas Attorney General Price Daniel, who had filed the initial *amicus curiae* intervention, ran for the United States Senate. On the promise that Daniel would again introduce a bill to return the tidelands to the states, Daniel beat incumbent Tom Connally in a hard-fought race. Texans knew Connally had betrayed them. Lyndon Johnson remained as Senate Majority

The Hot Oil War Goes National

Leader. Sam Rayburn was Speaker of the House. Texas would have clout in the halls of Congress. But the real leadership of Texas and the Democratic Party in Texas came from the governor.

The Democratic National Convention finally "drafted" Adlai Stevenson of Illinois to be its candidate. Stevenson's image with many Democratic voters was more than unappealing. It was appalling. He was the liberal's liberal, and reputed to be a poor judge of character.

On the floor of the convention, Shivers recognized that the tidelands and the federal assumption of power they represented were the only points worth discussing in this campaign. He flew to Springfield in August 1952 for a conference with the nominee.

They met face to face at "high noon." The streets might as well have been dusty and empty with Tex Ritter singing in the background. Shivers spent six or eight hours with Stevenson. In his holster was a carefully prepared brief on the tidelands, which he presented as a separate case. By 1952 no one doubted that the Gulf was rich in oil. More to the point, methods of recovering it had been devised and were constantly being improved.

Stevenson asked Shivers to give him time to study the brief. When Shivers came back, Stevenson said he would do as Truman had done, that is, he would veto any legislation to return the tidelands to the states.

For Shivers it was his defining moment. The press was waiting outside. Darkness was falling. Shivers made the statement carried on national radio and television that he could not support Stevenson for president. When the press later asked Stevenson his opinion, he seemed unconcerned. His answer was that if he were the Texas governor, he would probably do the same thing.

Stevenson misjudged the tidelands as a strictly Texas issue. Being from an inland state, he could not know the passions whipped to tornadic fury over a battle that had seesawed back and forth for seven years. His bad judgment proved to be the biggest mistake of his life.

Stevenson also misjudged the power and influence he was up against. He was sure he could win without Texas. The Republicans seemed deeply split over their nominee, General Dwight D. Eisenhower, a war hero who didn't seem deeply committed to running. The conservatives among the Republicans were already pointing privately to Richard Nixon, the vice-presidential running mate, as the man to carry the party next time around.

At the state convention in Amarillo, the majority was in favor of keeping Stevenson's name *off* the ballot. For the first time in a hundred years, Texas was not going to go Democratic. Shivers had promised at the National Convention to keep the ballot in its proper form. His speech won the day. He was their hometown boy, their cow town sheriff, their two-gun ranger, and their local hero.

And with him a new phenomenon was born, unique to Texas history and certainly rare in politics—the "Democrats for Eisenhower." Some called them "Shivercrats." Practically all the Democratic state officeholders from the governor on down cross-filed on the Republican ballot in the general election. Shivers' popularity was so great that he ran unopposed.

Oilmen hopped on the bandwagon early on when they learned that while the leases might cost them only twenty-five cents an acre, the federal government meant to require a 37½ percent oil royalty as on other federal property. The state had required producers to pay only 12½ percent royalty.

Texas liberals screamed and howled over Shivers' "sellout," but the battle cry that drowned them out was "Save the Tidelands for Our Children." Oil money whipped voters into a frenzy with advertising such as a beak-nosed Stevenson sneering at a classroom full of Texas children. "Tidelands funds for THOSE KIDS? Aw, let them pick cotton." The "Democrats for Eisenhower" raised more money for the Republican candidate in Texas than the Republican organization did nationwide.

Shivers polled 1,375,547 Democratic votes and 468,319 Republican votes for a total of 1,843,866 votes—by far the largest number of votes cast in Texas at that time. Eisenhower, the first Republican candidate since Reconstruction, carried the state with 53.1 percent of the votes.

Price Daniel easily defeated Tom Connally and was a key sponsor of a new Submerged Lands Act. Passed in 1953, it recognized the historic boundaries of *all* tidelands states. Eisenhower signed the act in 1953, and to this day Texas produces oil, gas, and sulfur from those lands.

It had been a long tough fight where three Supreme Court decisions were made against the states, three acts of Congress were passed in favor of the states, and two presidential vetoes went against the states. A major presidential campaign had turned on the issue, and a candidate had been defeated because of his stance against it.

Allan Shivers' father-in-law John Shary had died in 1945, leaving Shivers as general manager of the mammoth John H. Shary Enterprises—including 15,000 acres of fertile Rio Grande Valley land, nurseries, canneries, oil and gas property, banking interests, and a weekly newspaper. At the end of his term as governor in 1954, Shivers left public life. What his role in the history of the United States would have been is therefore open to speculation.

Certainly, anyone in Texas would have voted for him for whatever office he chose to campaign for. He might have been the only candidate in U.S. history to draw popular vote from both parties. In many ways he was a great loss to the country.

What Windfall Profits?

If the story of hot oil were to end with Allan Shivers and his triumphant return of the tidelands, what a wonderful and entertaining story the reader would have been treated to. Unfortunately, the tidelands were the high water mark for Texas oil. What follows is a tale of the near destruction of a proud independent industry that grew out of exploration and grinding labor, out of disappointment and triumph. As it unfolds, remember that for a short time, Texas oil made the United States number one in the world in oil production.

The tidelands became by act of Congress a part of Texas. The irony of the situation was that in the years that followed, the best oil strikes were found much farther out in the Gulf than three leagues. Although Texas did not receive what she had hoped from her political victory, she had acquired a good number of political debts.

Now it was payback time.

One payback came in the form of a reduction in the oil depletion allowance, a special tax break created specifically for oil; 27½ percent of any profit the industry made had been tax-free since 1913 when Calvin Coolidge had signed it into law. Big oil companies had pushed this benefit through Congress while locating oil was mostly guesswork and geologists were more interested in looking for veins of gold than seams of oil. The money that they had earned allowed men to keep on exploring and drilling until they "struck it rich" and to sustain their companies through the lean days of "dry holes."

The benefit had other economic advantages, more subtle and more widespread. It had come about when the industry needed an infusion of new capital. The law had the effect of creating a tax shelter for investors whose money was badly needed back in the days before World War I. It provided incentives for the rich man to subsidize the gambling wildcatters to keep on looking. It had nothing to do with the fact that all oil wells eventually were depleted (as many people believed).

Make no mistake. Until the huge East Texas lake blew in, the vast majority of wildcat wells came up dry, and as Spindletop proved, producing wells eventually stopped producing. Therefore, Texas oilmen believed unequivocally in the allowance. Many soon found they could not operate without it.

Another effort by the government to satisfy their voters had been price controls on oil and gas. So long as Spindletop was flowing and East Texas was heating up, gasoline was ten cents a gallon. Motorists loved the price. The infant automobile industry grew from a rich man's toy to a common man's necessity.

When oil production was brought under control, the price at the pump climbed. It was no longer ten cents a gallon. Yet people didn't want to pay more. If they had to pay more, they would not drive their cars so much. By that time the automobile industry, which also had powerful lobbyists in Washington, wanted people to trade in their huge gas-guzzling cars every two years. To make this constant swapping reasonable, families should be encouraged to put lots and lots of miles on their vehicles. The interstate highway system begun by Eisenhower beckoned.

Still, oil could make a man rich. An independent oilman who made a million dollars in a year could count on the first $275,000 to be tax free so he could keep on drilling.

In 1969 that began to change—swiftly. President Richard Nixon no longer looked with favor on this arrangement. He considered that Texas had abandoned him and his Republican bid for the White House against Kennedy and Johnson. The state under Allan Shivers had turned out for Eisenhower in 1952. Ike's vice president felt it should have turned out for him even against a favorite son.

And Congress—ever ready to discover more revenue to tax to support popular social programs begun by the Great Society—agreed with him.

In 1969 a bitter, vengeful man sat in the White House while Republicans in both houses of Congress were eager to get their hands on more revenue, especially if they could punish Texas in the process. The argument that ended the day for the oil depletion allowance was that all expenses for drilling were tax deductible from profits made when the oil came in. If the hole was dry, the oilman could still write off the expenses just as any other businessman did and slide into a lower tax bracket. Of course, if he drilled several dry holes, he might not have any more money, but perhaps he was in the wrong business. Though big oil howled, Congress lowered the depletion allowance to twenty-two percent.

In 1975 the depletion allowance for big oil was eliminated completely, and by 1984 the small producers were only allowed fifteen percent, with the promise that it would soon be ten percent.

So with prices kept artificially low and tax breaks and incentives eliminated, oilmen found themselves in a double bind—federal price controls and repeal of the depletion allowance.

It was—to all intents and purposes—the end of the independent oilman. He could no longer make a strike that would turn enough profit to make up for the losses incurred by the nine or ten wells that didn't come in. As Glenn McCarthy, one of the richest of the rich, asked, "If they're going to take all your money away from you when you make one well, and you're not going to recoup... the dry holes, how can you continue to operate?"

Still another problem loomed large. Texas was being drained of its wealth with nothing to repay it. The entire United States was running on Texas oil, yet Texas was having to *import* oil to keep its refineries going and paying for the oil it brought in from all over the world. Old oilmen, many of whom had been born between Spindletop and East Texas, faced the future with a sad pragmatism. Texas was going to be exhausted. No more oil fields were going to be found within her boundaries. The end was probably within sight.

At that time U.S. Senator Lloyd Bentsen, a conservative Texas Democrat, drove the nail in the coffin. He waged a presidential campaign pledging to cut the depletion allowance completely. He had betrayed his own people, but the betrayal did not profit him. Again Texas proved her power. Without his own state behind him, his campaign died.

Jimmy Carter of Georgia won the presidency from the Republicans, whose paranoid Nixon had led his administration into the Watergate scandal of rampant corruption, deceit, and illegality. In exchange for the Texas vote, Carter had promised that he would decontrol federal prices on oil and natural gas. However, in January 1977 one of the worst winters of the century brought oil and gas shortages. People were thrown out of work, and the words "energy crisis" were on everybody's lips.

Cast in the role of "the problem," Texas oil was forced again to remember "promises and piecrusts."

A National Energy Plan was unveiled. It amounted to a massive taxation program masquerading as conservation. One part of it kept price controls on oil while the government imposed a federal production tax to bring Texas prices to world levels. How this was supposed to happen was never made clear to anyone. As U.S. production dropped in the face of taxes, oil was imported as never before. In 1977 $44 billion worth of oil was imported as compared to $7.7 billion in 1973. The U.S. was more foreign oil dependent than ever, the exact opposite of what Carter had hoped to bring about.

In 1979 he announced a phased decontrol of U.S. crude oil prices. Unfortunately, it was accompanied by a new tax. The profit made by the decontrol was labeled a windfall rather than a fair recompense for all the oil that had been sold at bargain basement prices for two years.

It was deemed unexpected and unearned. Therefore, it should be taxed at a much higher rate. It was not even a tax on net income. It taxed the gross. Kept secret was the fact that it was not a tax on profits at all. It was merely labeled that so the country would see the oil companies as somehow bad and the government as somehow good. Most citizens were not aware that the nation imported any oil at all.

Lloyd Bentsen, now back in the Senate and suddenly on the other side of the fence called it, "one more sorry example of the government offering the carrot of decontrol and then taking it away with the stick of punitive taxation."

The exact description of the tax is a rigmarole of language, a sample of which follows: "The windfall profit on a barrel of crude oil was defined as the difference between the removal price of that barrel of crude oil on the one hand and the sum of the adjusted base price of that oil under prior regulation plus the severance tax adjustment on the other. It taxed upper and lower tiered oil, newly termed tier 1 oil, at the rate of 70 percent; stripper oil, newly termed tier 2 oil, at the rate of 50 percent; and newly discovered oil, some heavy oils of sixteen-degree gravity or below, and oil from tertiary recovery, all termed tier 3 oil, at 30 percent." Readers wishing to know more about this should consult Commerce Clearing House, *Crude Oil Windfall Profit Tax of 1980,* pp. 1-15.

Some of the old hot oil wars began again, as tier 1 oil was moved under cover of darkness or by secret pipelines to tertiary discovery sites, but the hearts of the oilmen weren't in it. They were older and more discouraged. They could see no end in sight, no return to the "good old days."

Moreover, the situation had become so complicated that oil companies big and small were literally drowning under a sea of paperwork. Though prices were much higher than they were when hot oil was running out of East Texas, there was really very little more profit.

One small operator summed matters up. "You know, I get roughly $8,000 a month, and if I don't work it right close, I write $9,000 worth of checks paying bills. Where the hell is that big windfall profit?"

At the same time prices at the pump were not allowed to rise as they should have. People were restless. Carter's administration did not want them upset. Indeed the president wanted the population to conserve because the situation in the Middle East was heating up.

As a matter of economic law, imposing price controls never inspires conservation. Instead they make things worse sometimes in unexpected ways. When the Carter administration sought to hold down the price of oil and make the United States less dependent on foreign oil, its efforts resulted in the opposite effect. It could do nothing about the import of cheap foreign oil, so it held down the price of domestic oil. As domestic supplies fell short, as fewer and fewer companies sold their oil, more and more foreign oil came in to meet the country's needs. From 1975 to 1979—amid exhortations that everyone conserve fuel—imports rose from thirty-three percent to nearly fifty percent of total consumption. The United States became more dependent rather than less.

Congress facilitated the process through the "Oil Entitlements Program," which was set to subsidize small refineries but ended up subsidizing oil imports. Consumers who were "entitled" to cheap oil had their prices supported. Soon the foreigners sold their oil at higher supported prices than they would otherwise have been paid.

More and more oil was sold to the United States, stretching world supplies so tight that when the Shah of Iran fell in 1979 and American hostages were imprisoned in their own embassy in Teheran, American motorists sat in their cars in gas lines—odd license numbers on odd days of the week, even on even.

A surprise collateral damage was done to the auto industry. Overconfidence that gas prices would be stabilized had cut the introduction of the Chevette and other economy cars between 1975 and 1979. When the whole country decided to buy new fuel-efficient models during three short months in 1979, the auto companies were caught short. They were then blamed for "not producing fuel-efficient cars."

The Carter administration was making plans to regulate the auto industry when the hostage situation drove them out of office in 1980.

Despite new discoveries and new and improved production methods, the United States has never recovered its supremacy in the world of oil. Saudi Arabia is number one along with a host of small countries with which the United States maintains shaky diplomatic relations.

The situation is as unstable as it has ever been as gas prices climb every summer.

The Hot Oil War Goes International

"The U.S. has a disproportionate responsibility for the freedom and the security of various countries. And a lot of what is at stake in the Gulf relates to that."

George Herbert Walker Bush— the Hot Oil President

Texas *Politicians: Good 'n' Bad* cannot end without a few words about the Bush family. The former and current presidents of the United States both claim Texas as their home because Texas was where they made their fortunes. As one might expect—they made them in oil.

George Herbert Walker Bush is the son of a Wall Street banker and U.S. Senator from Connecticut. He was born to wealth and privilege, though he has often said that the privilege came "from having parents that teach you values." He was the youngest navy pilot in World War II, where he flew in the Pacific theatre. He was shot down and rescued at sea. After the war he married Barbara, graduated Phi Beta Kappa in economics from Yale, and then refused to join his father's firm.

Instead he went to Texas to make a career in the Permian Basin oil fields, specifically Midland, where his son George W. was born. High-grade crude oil was discovered through deep testing where oil—if it were present—was unrecoverable by drillers in the first half of the century. Since timing is everything, the elder George's timing was impeccable. Within a relatively short time—less than twenty years—he had made a fortune there and offshore in the Gulf of Mexico.

No longer needing to work to earn a living, he decided thereafter to devote himself to politics as a servant of the people. In 1964 he lost a race for the Senate, and in 1966 he won a seat to the U.S. Congress. There he discovered his real interest was not sitting among the many. He preferred to be on his own. He sought and received the position of U.S. Ambassador to the United Nations in 1971. He served as U.S. envoy to China in 1974. In 1975 he became director of the CIA.

His interest was international. More than any other U.S. president, he had connections and experience abroad before he came to the presidential chair. He hoped to be nominated for president in 1980. When Ronald Reagan won the Republican nomination, he tapped Bush for vice president. In 1988 Bush was nominated for president and won with Reagan's endorsement.

Throughout his term he was more successful in foreign affairs than domestic. During his term the Soviet Union collapsed, and as one communist government after another was swept away, he became increasingly popular. Though he was forced to raise taxes despite promising not to, the voters forgave him—for a few months. The reason for this unprecedented spike in popularity was Operation Desert Storm.

It was what the British officers of Victoria's empire would once have termed "a bloody-damned good war." Long enough to earn some combat stripes and make some heroes, short enough that almost nobody got hurt. It made heroes out of

Generals Norman Schwarzkopf and Colin Powell. It lasted for nearly a year in diplomatic maneuvering where George Bush proved his worth in dealing with the last premier of the Soviet Union—Mikhail Gorbachev.

When Iraqi dictator Saddam Hussein refused to withdraw his invading troops from Kuwait, the hot oil war became a major plot for the news as entertainment industry. United States and the world were treated via the medium of television to the green skies over Baghdad alight with the trails of smart bombs streaking to their targets. Patriot missiles took out SCUDS. An audience in Israel wore gas masks to a cello concert. It was high drama.

The desert a hundred miles from Baghdad was the scene of a 100-hour land campaign where ill-equipped, unsupported Iraqi soldiers surrendered in droves to American soldiers as television cameras showed their mercy and forbearance to their enemies and to the world. So bold and so news hungry did the networks become that one television crew went out and captured their own Iraqis so that they could have an exclusive. So eager were the soldiers to be captured that no one noticed until the crew brought their prisoners in that enemy soldiers still had weapons in their hands.

Only 144 Americans were killed. It had everything: heroes and heroines, a smarmy villain, a righteous cause, and spectacle. It was the ultimate hot oil war taken international.

Justification for the taking up of arms came when Saddam Hussein ordered the Kuwaiti oil fields set afire. The deliberate destruction of such a valuable resource demonized the dictator forever in the eyes of the international community. Only a few rogue nations could find anything good to say about such wanton waste and pollution of the environment of both the neighboring nations and the skies, waters, and shores of the rivers of the Fertile Crescent and the Persian Gulf.

Bush's approval rating stood at 91 percent, the highest of any American president. People were proud to be Americans.

It began to drop as he drew criticism for ending Desert Storm too soon, but he was also able to strike a peaceful agreement with new Russian president Boris Yeltsin for the official end of the Cold War. At the same time the Berlin Wall came down. Again millions of television viewers saw each event: Yeltsin waving the flag of free Russia in front of the Kremlin and Berliners taking out their frustrations with sledgehammers on the wall that had divided the city for so long.

Still, with all this success abroad, nothing seemed to go right at home. Riots erupted in Los Angeles. A third party candidate, Ross Perot, entered the presidential race, splitting the votes of each party enough to give the presidency to Bill Clinton in 1993.

What do people say about George Bush today? His presidency is looked back on rather fondly as a time of dignity and respect. No one can doubt that it was a time when a man did the best job he could and did it with honor.

The future waits upon his son George W. Bush, who vaulted from the Texas governor's chair to the Oval Office in three short years. Texas now can boast of only the second father and son combination in our nation's history.

For better or for worse, Texas politicians now dominate the world.

Bibliography

"Allred, James Burr V" *The Handbook of Texas Online.* http://www.tsha.utexas.edu/handbook/online/articles/view/AA/fal42.html [Accessed Mon Apr 30 13:25:40 US/Central 2001].

Anderson, James E., *et al. Texas Politics: An Introduction.* New York: Harper & Row, 1979.

"Bailey, Joseph Weldon." *The Handbook of Texas Online.* http://www.tsha.utexas.edu/handbook/online/articles/view/BB/fba10.html [Accessed Sun Apr 15 14:13:40 US/Central 2001].

Banks, Jimmy. *Money, Marbles and Chalk: The Wondrous World of Texas Politics.* Austin: Texas Publishing Co., 1971.

"Barker Texas History Center." *The Handbook of Texas Online.* http://www.tsha.utexas.edu/handbook/online/articles/view/BB/lch1.html [Accessed Thu Feb 22 6:01:02 US/Central 2001].

Benton, Wilbourn E. *Texas: Its Government and Politics.* Third Edition. New Jersey: Prentice-Hall, Inc., 1972.

Biffle, Kent. *A Month of Sundays.* Denton: University of North Texas Press, 1993.

Bolton, Paul. *Governors of Texas.* The San Angelo Standard-Times, 1947.

Clark, John E. *The Fall of the Duke of Duval: A Prosecutor's Journal.* Austin: Eakin Press, 1999.

Conkin, Paul K. *Big Daddy from the Pedernales: Lyndon Baines Johnson.* Boston: Twayne Publishers, 1986.

Cotner, Robert C. *James Stephen Hogg, A Biography.* Austin: University of Texas Press, 1959.

Crawford, Anne Fears and Crystal Sasse Ragsdale. *Women in Texas: Their Lives, Their Experiences, Their Accomplishments.* Austin: State House Press, 1992.

Davidson, Chandler. *Race and Class in Texas Politics.* Princeton: Princeton University Press, 1990.

DeShields, James T. *They Sat in High Places: The Presidents and Governors of Texas.* San Antonio: Naylor, 1940.

Durant, Will. *The Story of Philosophy: The Lives and Opinions of the Greater Philosophers.* New York: Simon and Schuster, 1951.

Farrell, Mary D. and Elizabeth Silverthorne. *First Ladies of Texas: The First One Hundred Years.* Belton, Texas: Stillhouse Hollow, 1976.

Fehrenbach, T. R. *Lone Star: A History of Texas and the Texans.* New York: The Macmillan Company, 1968.

"Ferguson Forum." *The Handbook of Texas Online.* http://www.tsha.utexas.edu/handbook/online/articles/view/FF/eef2/html [Accessed Wed Jan 31 13:42:43 US/Central/2001].

"Ferguson, James Edward." *The Handbook of Texas Online.* http://www.tsha.utexas.edu/handbook/online/articles/view/FF/ffe5.html [Accessed Wed Jan 31 13:45:46 US/Central 2001].

"Former County Judge Dies." *Valley Morning Star,* November 4, 2000.

Gantt, Fred Jr., ed., et al. *Governing Texas: Documents and Readings.* Third Edition. New York: Thomas Y. Crowell Company, 1974.

Henninger, Daniel, "Common-Sense Government in Only 100 Days," *The Wall Street Journal*, April 26, 2001, A20.

Knowles, Ruth Sheldon. *The Greatest Gamblers: The Epic of American Oil Exploration.* 2nd Ed. Norman: University of Oklahoma Press, 1978.

Kunhardt, Philip B. *et al. The American President.* New York: Riverhead Books, 1999.

Malavis, Nicholas George. *Bless the Pure and Humble: Texas Lawyers and Oil Regulation, 1919-1936.* College Station: Texas A&M University Press, 1996.

Morehead, Richard. *50 Years in Texas Politics—From Roosevelt to Reagan—From the Fergusons to Clements.* Burnet, Texas: The Eakin Press, 1982.

Nevin, David. *The Texans.* Revised edition. Alexandria, Virginia: Time/Life Books, 1982.

"Oil and Gas Industry." *The Handbook of Texas Online.* http://www.tsha.utexas.edu/handbook/online/articles/view/OO/doogz/html [Accessed Mon Apr 30 13:42:27 UX/Central 2001].

Olien, Roger M. and Diana Davids Olien. *Life in the Oil Fields.* Austin: Texas Monthly Press, 1986.

_____. *Wildcatters: Texas Independent Oilmen.* Austin: Texas Monthly Press, 1984.

Paulissen, Maisie. "Pardon Me, Governor Ferguson," in *Legendary Ladies of Texas,* edited by Francis Edward Abernathy. Dallas: E-Heart Press, 1981.

Presley, James. *A Saga of Wealth: The Rise of the Texas Oilmen.* Austin: Texas Monthly Press, 1983.

Sheehy, Sandy. *Texas Big Rich.* New York: William Morrow and Co., 1990.

Shivers, Allan. "The Governor's Office in Retrospect," in *Governing Texas: Documents and Readings* edited by Fred Gantt Jr. *et al.* New York: Thomas Crowell, 1974.

"Shivers, Robert Allan." *The Handbook of Texas Online.* http://www.tsha.utexas.edu/handbook/online/articles/view/SS/fsh40.html [Accessed Mon Apr 30 13:30:17 US/Central 2001].

Simpson, Glenn R. and Evan Perez. "Tainted Returns," *The Wall Street Journal,* December 19, 2000.

"Sterling, Ross Shaw." *The Handbook of Texas Online.* http://www.tsha.utexas.edu/handbook/online/articles/view/SS/fst42.html [Accessed Tue Apr 17 13:26:00US/Central 2001].

"Tidelands Controversy." *The Handbook of Texas Online.* http://www.tsha.utexas.edu/handbook/online/articles/view/TT/mgt2.html [Accessed Mon Apr 30 13:34:16 US/Central 2001].

Texas Almanac 2000-2001. Dallas: The Dallas Morning News, 1999.

Tucker, William. "California's Price Caps Aren't Likely to Stay 'Temporary,'" *The Wall Street Journal,* May 2, 2001, A32.

Welch, June Rayfield. *The Texas Governors.* Dallas: G. L. A. Press, 1977.

Index

A
Acero, Mrs. Enriqueto, 59
ad valorem taxes, 17-18
Alaniz, Nago, 64-65
Allee, Alfred Y., 65-66
Allred, James V, 198-201, 203-205
automobile industry, 218, 223-224

B
Bailey, Joseph Weldon, 157-170
  bank closing, 42
  photo, 158
  scandals, 168-170
Bateman, Ed, 186
Bentsen, Lloyd, 219-220
Black, Justice Hugo, 60, 211
Bradford, Daisy, 178, 181-184
Brown and Root Construction Company, 86, 90-91
Bush, George Herbert Walker, 223-226
Bush, George W., 47, 224, 226
Butte, Dr. George, 33, 177

C
Carter, Jimmy, 219-222
Clark, George, 137-139 162-163
Clark, Tom, 212
Collier's, 62
Connally, John, 68 109-110
Connally, Tom, 199
Constitution of 1875, 47
conversion of transportation to oil, 155
Corsicana oil strike, 140-141
Crim, Lou Della, 178, 186
Cullinan, "Buckskin Joe," 141, 149, 151-152, 174

D
Daniel, Price, 210, 212, 215
Davis, E. J., 28, 47 131
Democratic National Convention, 75
dependence on foreign oil, 223-224

E
East Texas Oil Field, 186
education reforms, 17
Eisenhower, Dwight, 213-214
Equal Employment Opportunities Commission, 107-109

F
Farish, William S., 172-173, 176, 202
farm problem, 12-17
Ferguson Nalle, Ouida, 10, 23-24, 30, 41
Ferguson, James "Farmer Jim," 7-12, 15-22, 38, 43, 87, 92

Index

Ferguson Forum, 20
friendship with archer parr, 52
impeachment, 19
photo, 9, 41
Ferguson, Miriam "Ma," 7-8, 10, 18, 21, 23-45, 54-55, 58, 87, 92, 94, 100, 171, 176-177, 194, 198-199
campaigns, 26, 27, 31-33, 39
closing the banks, 42
photo, 25, 41
quoted in *Ferguson Forum,* 24
Ford, Rip, 47
Francis, David R., 161
Freedom Party, 62-66, 72

G

Gates, "Bet-a-Million," 152
Gonzaulles, Sergeant Manuel T. "Lone Wolf," 192-194
Gould, Jay, 129-130, 132, 134-135, 156
"Great Society," 112-114, 116
Guffey Petroleum Company, 149

H

Hamill, Al, 144-145, 147
Hamill, Curt, 145
Hamill, Jim, 144
Hamm, W. D., 181
Higgins, Patillo, 143, 147
Hobby, William, 20, 33
Hogg, Ima, 152, 168-169
Hogg, James Stephen, 129-130, 154, 164-169, 175
death, 168-169
Hogg-Swayne Syndicate, 149-151

war on corporations, 133-135, 143
"hot oilers," 190-192, 194, 199, 221-222
Houston Post, 39
Humble Oil and Refining Company, 39, 172
Hunt, Haroldson Lafayette, 186
Hussein, Saddam, 227

I

Ickes, Harold L., 55, 194, 200, 202, 206, 211
Independent Petroleum Association of Texas, 187

J

Johnson, Lady Bird, 81-83, 90-91, 93, 98, 100, 106-107, 113, 117-119
Johnson, Lyndon Baines, 5, 66-69, 72-120
action in World War II, 88-90
background, 77-79
Box 13, 57-60, 95-97
campaigns, 83-86, 93
health, 68-69, 84, 92-93, 101, 116-117, 119
marries Lady Bird, 81-82
photo, 85, 94, 99, 110, 115, 119
purchases the LBJ Ranch, 100
Senate Majority Leader, 101-104
vice president, 105-109
Joiner, Columbus Marion "Dad," 179-185
Jones, Jesse, 84

K

Kennedy, Jacqueline, 107, 110
Kennedy, John F., 67-68, 73-77, 105-107, 109
  assassination, 68, 110-111
Kennedy, Robert, 68-69, 118
King Jr., Martin Luther, 118, 199
King Ranch, 53
Kleberg, Richard Mifflin, 55-56, 61, 73, 79-81
Kleberg, Robert, 53, 56
Ku Klux Klan, 21, 26-30, 33-34, 46
  Anti-mask bill, 36-37
  Texas attitude toward, 28

L

Laster, Ed, 181-183
LBJ Ranch, 100
Lloyd, Dr. A. C. "Doc," 179-181
Lucas, Captain Anthony, 128, 142-144, 147
Lyle, John E. Jr., 56
  photo, 142

M

McCarthy hearings, 103
McCarthy, Glenn, 219
Moody, Dan, 38, 176

N

Nixon, Richard, 76, 77, 217-218

O

O'Daniel, W. Lee "Pappy," 42-43, 85, 92
oil and gas legislation, 174-175, 190
oil depletion allowance, 217-219
oil discovery and business, 123-128
  laws, 125-127
  sales of leases, 148
  waste and exploitation, 148, 150, 153
oil prices, 189
oil regulation, 200-202
Old Party, 63, 68, 72
Operation Desert Storm, 226-227

P

pardoning of criminals, 18, 37-38, 44
Parr, Archer (Archie), 19, 38, 44, 47-53
  election of Lyndon Johnson, 45
  paternalism, 50-51
  rules of power, 49
Parr, Archer (young "Archie"), 66, 68
Parr, George, 52-72, 94, 96
  assets, 62
  death, 70-72
  federal prisoner, 54
  IRS investigation, 53, 55, 69
  pardoned by Truman, 57
Parr, Givens, 52
Parr, Thelma Duckworth, 61
Pearl Harbor, 88
Perry, Governor Rick, 47
Pierce, Henry Clay, 160, 162-165, 167
poll tax, 16, 49-50, 62
Pratt, Wallace, 173, 174
prorationing, 187, 188

Index

R

Rayburn, Sam, 76, 84, 90, 92, 98, 199
Reagan, John H., 136
Richards, Ann, 36
Robertson, Felix, 21, 26, 28-29, 31, 33
Rockefeller, John D., 156
Roosevelt, Franklin D., 40, 56, 87, 90 199
Ross, Nellie Tayloe, 33
Russell, Richard, 98, 114

S

science of oil production, 202-205
Shivers, Robert Allan, 5, 63, 206-208, 213-216
  photo, 207
  "Shivercrats," 214
Spindletop, 146-147, 153-157, 186, 172, 187
Standard Oil, 141, 143, 156, 159-163, 175-176
State Democratic Convention, 164
Stautz, Carl, 69
Sterling, Ross Shaw, 38-39, 171-196
  newspapers, 176
  photo, 178
Stevenson, Adlai, 213-214
Stevenson, Coke, 44-45, 56-60, 86-87, 92, 94-97

T

Texas Traffic Association, 134
Texas Railroad Commission, 135-136, 140, 153, 156, 167, 175, 188, 193, 202
  Duties, 187-188
Texas Rangers, 38-39, 65
tidelands controversy, 208-214
  suit against Texas, 212
Truman, Harry S., 56, 92, 208, 210-212

U

University of Texas, 19, 34

V

Vietnam War, 114, 117

W

Warren, Chief Justice Earl, 113
Waters-Pierce Oil Company, 160-170
  monopoly and conspiracy against trade, 159-161
Wells, Jim, 39
windfall profits tax, 221
Wolters, General Jacob, 190-191
woman suffrage, 18, 23, 24, 27
Wood, Nola, 36
Woodbine sand, 186
Wrather, Jack D., 194

Other titles by Mona D. Sizer

The King Ranch Story: Truth and Myth
1-55622-680-2 • $16.95

Texas Heroes A Dynasty of Courage
1-55622-775-2 • $18.95

Texas Justice, Bought and Paid For
1-55622-791-4 • $18.95

Looking for more?

Check out these and other great

In the Boat with LBJ
John L. Bullion

J.W. Bullion refers to his experience working for Lyndon Johnson as a tax attorney and business advisor as "being in the boat." LBJ was the captain; the crew either met his standards for effort and excellence or they got out. This book describes the impact of being in the boat with LBJ and contains many accounts of LBJ at his beloved ranch on the Pedernales.

1-55622-880-5 • $21.95

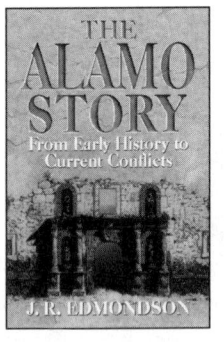

The Alamo Story From Early History to Current Conflicts
J.R. Edmondson

Impeccably researched history that reads like a novel, J.R. Edmondson's work is justifiably the successor to *A Time to Stand*, and will continue to set the new standard for Alamo history books for years to come.

1-55622-678-0 • $24.95

Texas Bad Boys: Gamblers, Gunfighters, and Grifters
J. Lee Butts

This book takes the reader back to those lethal days of yesteryear for a vivid picture of the most feared man-killers who ever walked the dusty streets of the real Texas frontier. From the 1840s right up until yesterday's headlines, killers, con men, and reprobates of every stripe come back to life and rip through the pages of this new book from the author of *Texas Bad Girls*.

1-55622-879-1 • $18.95

Lone Star Ladies: A Travel Guide to Women's History in Texas
Melinda Rice

Exploring the places in Texas devoted to its daughters—from Babe Didrikson Zaharias and Bonnie Parker to the Women Airforce Service Pilots, this book crisscrosses the state in search of women's history. Each section includes biographies, directions to each site, hours and fees, maps and pictures, and a statewide cross-reference for easy trip planning.

1-55622-847-3 • $18.95

For more information visit us online at

titles from Republic of Texas Press

The Courage of Common Men: Texans Remember World War II
Stephen Neal Manning

These interviews with a collection of World War II veterans from across Texas tell stories of tragedy, romance, and humor. Included are cherished photographs of the veterans during the war and as they are now.

1-55622-838-4 • $18.95

Tales From Out Yonder
Ross McSwain

A mixture of stories about Texas people, places, and things, from frontiersman-rancher-fugitive Humpy Jackson, who drove Col. Ronald Mackenzie and his soldiers crazy, to the first emperor to visit America. Other stories include the ghost of the Brambletye mansion, Pancho Villa's war for the movie cameras, and much more.

1-55622-848-1 • $18.95

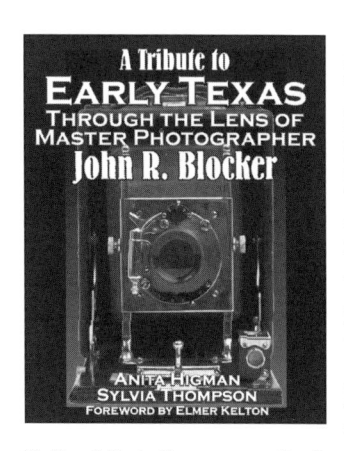

A Tribute to Early Texas—Through the Lens of Master Photographer John R. Blocker
Anita Higman and Sylvia Thompson

This collection of black and white photos by John R. Blocker from the 1920s to the 1940s truly captures the essence of Texas including Big Bend before it became a National Park, the preservation longhorn herd, the building of the Texas dams, the missions, creeks, windmills, wildflowers. The book also includes an index and a foreword by Elmer Kelton.

1-55622-837-6 • $21.95

www.republicoftexaspress.com